NEW LIFE
FOR YOUR
CHURCH

Dale Young

Phoenix, AZ

March 1991

NEW LIFE
FOR YOUR
CHURCH

A Renewal Handbook for Pastors

DOYLE L. YOUNG

BAKER BOOK HOUSE
Grand Rapids, Michigan 49516

To the Tuesday-morning group,
which now meets on Thursday.

Woe to you who are complacent in Zion . . . .
You will be among the first to go into exile;
Your feasting and lounging will end.

Amos 6:1, 7

Help, LORD, for the godly are no more;
The faithful have vanished from among men.

Psalm 12:1

"No one puts new wine into old wineskins;
If he does, the wine will burst the skins,
and both wine and the wineskins will be ruined.
No, he pours new wine into new wineskins."

Mark 2:22

Contents

Preface

There is no expectation that all of my opinions will be well received by my readers; I do hope, however, that they will spark thought and study.

These principles are applicable in any Christian context, regardless of form (local congregation, military chapel, a missionary field) or denomination. Though my own background has been somewhat provincial, these ideas, I believe, are not.

One final observation remains. This short work is not an exercise in ivory-tower reflection. At this writing I have been a seminary professor for five years; for nearly three of these years I have also served as pastor of a vibrant congregation. The Greenwood Baptist Church of Weatherford, Texas, is a seventy-five-year old, semirural fellowship which has, in five years' time, more than doubled in size. It has been in this loving fellowship that many of these theoretical ideas have taken on flesh. Our church certainly is not ideal or perfect, and we did not in three years implement all these ideas; but they have been in our minds while we have sought the Spirit's guidance as to how we should go. (In this book the local church is distinguished from the universal Church by the capitalization of the body of Christ: Church.)

Introduction

In ancient Egyptian mythology is the story of the phoenix, a fabulous bird. As large as an eagle, with scarlet and gold feathers, the phoenix had a beautiful cry. Only one phoenix lived at a time and its lifespan was very long. As the phoenix's death approached, it would build a nest of boughs and spices, set it on fire, and then be consumed in the flames. As the old phoenix died, from the fire and ashes there would arise a new phoenix. In this miraculous rebirth new life sprang from death.

At the risk of sounding apocalyptic, I suggest that Western Christianity may be in its death throes. The flames are leaping around the pyre. The institutional Church may well be breathing its last, in the ashes, struggling to rise and take new flight. I am not alone in this assessment.

The late David Watson wrote that the struggle of the twenty-first century will be between Marxism, Islam, and Third-World Christianity. Western Christianity, he declared, is too weak to be of help.[1]

Howard Snyder suggests "perhaps Western culture is nearing a point where the Christian faith can be successfully reintroduced. Maybe the collapse of the present order will lead to a new outbreak of revolutionary Christianity."[2]

Donald Bloesch has spoken out

> . . . in a time when the moral and spiritual foundations of West-
> ern culture are collapsing. The temptation to despair is almost
> overwhelming when we stop to consider how the church is com-
> promising with a cultural ethos that is becoming ever more fla-
> grantly pagan. . . . the real enemy is not the humanistic heritage
> of the Enlightenment (though this remains an adversary of the
> Christian faith) but an aggressive paganism and nihilism that
> deny even the moral norms that the Enlightenment refused to
> jettison. . . .[3]

"We find ourselves today," Bloesch continues, "in a cultural
situation in which historical Christianity appears to be in
eclipse."[4] And to those who trumpet the apparent success
of conservative evangelicalism (for example, in national
politics or television programs), Bloesch suggests that such
apparent success "may also be an Indian summer before
the total collapse of organized religion in this country."[5]

Is there any evidence for such an analysis? Yes. The situation in Europe is nearing disastrous proportions.[6] In
England, only 6 percent of the population regularly attend
worship services, while the figures are worse elsewhere:
Australia (4 percent), West Germany-East Germany-Scan-
dinavia (4 percent or less), and in Madrid, Spain, (3-5 percent). Among church members in West Germany, only two-
thirds believe in God and only one-third accept the resur-
rection of Jesus. Less than half of Dutch Catholics believe
that Jesus was divine, and still fewer believe in life after
death. In 1976, only 29 percent of Britain's population believed in a personal God (down from 38 percent in 1963).
Only 7.6 percent of Japanese youth have any kind of religious belief and only 9 percent of Brazilians are practicing
Catholics (versus 33 percent who are practicing Spiritists).

Half of the Methodist churches in England have fewer
than twenty-five in worship, while the Church of Scotland
has declined in membership by one-third in sixteen years.
Though 90 percent of French citizens have a Catholic back-

ground, only 15 percent regularly attend church, and only 36 percent of French citizens believe in God. Another study notes that only 4 percent of the French population accepts the idea of sin. The decline of vocations to the priesthood in the Roman Catholic Church is universal but particularly acute in France: over one thousand parishes have no pastor.

The American picture appears only somewhat brighter. The mainline denominations continue their decline (though at a slower rate). Some evangelical groups are showing modest gains.[7] But a 1983 Gallup poll reported that only 12 percent of the U.S. population considers itself "highly committed" to religious practice.[8] Further, countries which show a higher interest in religion (Poland, Northern Ireland, USA) reveal, upon examination, a wedding of nationalistic and cultural goals with Christianity; these Christian groups serve as a support for the culture's values and goals.[9]

In the USA, Sunday-school enrollment declined over 34 percent between 1970 and 1986, and in those same years the percentage of people who said that they received no religious training as a child increased from 10 percent to 27 percent.[10] Southern Baptists, traditionally an evangelistic and fast-growing American group, saw the number of baptisms in their churches level off in the mid-1980s, and a Southern Baptist executive dismally reported that 50 percent of those whom Southern Baptists do baptize drop out of active church life.[11] Further, on the last Sunday of the 1986 church year (September), of the 14.6 million Southern Baptist church members, only 3.9 million were in Sunday school and only 4.8 million attended worship.[12]

We live in apocalyptic days. And we ask "What's happening?" "What's wrong with the Church?"

What is happening is rather clear. The Church is in serious trouble because it has compromised itself. We have been captured by our culture. We practice an insipid, anemic Christianity that accepts and applauds our cultural values and norms. Radical—that is, *biblical*—Christianity, is rarely seen in our midst. What now passes for "radical

Christianity" is often a bizarre subjectivism that is no closer
to the early Church's way than is the domesticated Christianity of the established denominations.

This cultural captivity of the Church is seen first in a
general secularization. The Church in the West now regularly follows cultural fads and values. The current issues for
many progressive denominations are women's rights, gay
rights, and the peace movement, all dictated by the "liberal"
wing of the culture. For the more conservative groups the
issues are science versus religion, strong military defense,
and maintaining traditional American values; these issues
are dictated by the society's "conservative" wing. The point
is this: society sets the agenda, and the churches usually
endorse and defend some set of *cultural* (not *biblical*) values.
Bloesch puts it clearly: the "liberal" denominations are captive to the ideological left, while the "conservative" denominations are captive to the ideological right.[13] The voice of
God is muffled by the layers of cultural accretions in the
churches. For the doubters among you, try an experiment:
voice in a "conservative" church a "liberal" political idea
(or vice versa) and gauge the reaction.

Our cultural captivity is further seen in the churches'
unmitigated acceptance of a brazen, unrepentant materialism. One only has to open one's eyes to see that the high-
est American value (materialism) has become the ultimate
value in many of our churches. By building ever larger, ever
more luxurious buildings, we have announced our rejection of biblical teaching in favor of what our society says
is important. We follow a corporate model for the employ-
ment, organization, and compensation of employees (ministers). And we define success the same way the world
does: more, bigger, better. Like American business, we
have become utilitarian: whatever works to reach our goals
must be right. We haven't stopped to ask if our *goals* are
right, or our *methods*. One will rarely hear a pastor who is
paid sixty thousand dollars a year stand in a sanctuary that

cost 15 million dollars and denounce, as did Amos, the flagrant materialism of the day.

Our cultural captivity is also seen in our nationalism. Now, before you assume that I'm a left-wing Red, let me answer you that I am an officer (chaplain) in the U.S. Air Force Reserve and have been for eight years. I am on twenty-four hour notice to report for active duty in the event of a national crisis, so I don't want to be chastised for "not being patriotic."

But though I respect my country and I "give to Caesar what is Caesar's," I will not give to Caesar "what is God's"— that is, my ultimate allegiance. The rise of a militant nationalism has been swallowed and endorsed in many churches. People believe that the USA does no wrong. Christian people even assert that "the American Way" (American values, goals, foreign-policy objectives, economic progress) is "God's way." This blatant baptizing of what is often the baldest American selfishness is nothing less than blasphemy. If one believes that this country has a right to do whatever she wishes and can get away with, that's one's opinion; but we drag God into it and say that that is what *he* wants. This "enthronement of the state or nation"[14] receives the support of many Christians.

What has been the result of this process of secularization and cultural captivity? The Church has lost its identity and mission. The world has shaped us and caused us to forget who we are and what we are to do. Though maintaining all the outward forms of religion, we are sinking into the ashes.

What, then, can we do? Can the phoenix rise from the ashes into new life? Can we avoid despair and total capitulation to the culture?

There *is* a path to new life in the Church. It is not an easy way, for it goes against the grain of established church life. The travelers on this road will be considered malcontents, troublemakers, people with an attitude problem. We must tread this way, however, for the alternative (status quo, business as usual) is too serious to imagine. To avoid becoming an even more irrelevant curiosity, the people of Christ must move ahead. We must face the truth about our world, our churches, and ourselves. We must walk the narrow way of real obedience and discipleship.

Is there a plan for how to do this? There is. It is this:

We have too often simply tinkered with new methods without first rethinking more foundational things. This model suggests that we must first define *who* we (the Church) are. We can then discern the Church's *tasks* in the world. Then, with our identity and tasks clearly seen, we can enunciate *principles* to shape our church life. The last step, finally, is to discuss *methods* and techniques that are appropriate for our day.

1

How I Got Here

or
My Descent into the Ashes

To be perfectly honest, the Church has, for most of my adult life, irritated, bored, angered, or depressed me. Only rarely—but often enough to keep me returning—have I seen the flashes of the Holy Spirit's reality and power. In the throes of youthful idealism, I was aghast to find the community of Christ's people to be also thoroughly human, petty, selfish, and sinful; it helped somewhat to find that this description included me as well.

Really it didn't help much, for simply to recognize that Christians are yet humans didn't answer the questions "Is the Church on the right track?" or "How would we know it if we *were* on the right track?"

My dissatisfaction—my sense of things not being quite right—reached a critical stage in 1983-85, when I was at the age of thirty to thirty-two (students of developmental psychology will be permitted a knowing smile). The sobering thought occurred to me that I, a child of Southern Baptist churches all my life, youth-group leader, holder of four theological degrees from Southern Baptist schools, former youth minister, former university minister, former pastor, former college Bible instructor, seminary professor, published scholar, and U. S. Air Force Reserve chaplain, had really very little clear idea what the local church or ministry was supposed to be and do, or how to evaluate what we in that church were being and doing. I had virtually no conception of the universal Church's soul.

If this is taken as an indictment of my evangelical upbringing and theological education, let it be one without rancor. I happily concede that the fault may have been largely mine, for I was not seeking in those years to grapple with the Church's identity and task. But I must also assert that nowhere, as I remember, was I ever challenged or encouraged to grapple with these issues, and this, it seems to me now, *must be* an integral part of Christian maturity and, certainly, of theological education. I was, by age twenty-eight, privy to the secrets of the most deep theology and well versed in the traditional, functional methods and techniques of evangelical church life. But there was yet a sense of something wrong—of jumping ahead too far—of learning about and debating the latest techniques without first having laid the theological and pastoral foundations. We seemed to be stumbling around in the darkness. For me, church life raced past "discouraging" to "infuriating."

I don't remember how I first bumped into the wide literature of what is called "the church-renewal movement," or even of the progression of the writers I discovered. Twenty-five years before my "time of questioning," eloquent, thoughtful writers began addressing the same questions. Elton Trueblood is, I suppose, the "father" of the movement in America. Others who influenced me deeply in my personal and ecclesial quest were John Claypool (one of my role models since college days), and Michael Green (formerly of Saint Aldate's Church, Oxford, England, and now of Regent College, Vancouver, British Columbia). Other tributaries into my "stream" were Henri Nouwen of Yale (and a Roman Catholic priest), Scott Peck (a practicing psychiatrist), Richard Foster (of Friends University), Edith Schaeffer (of L'Abri Fellowship in Switzerland), Jim Wallis (of the Sojourners Community in Washington D.C.), Elizabeth O'Connor (of the Church of the Savior in Washington, D.C.), Keith Miller (an Episcopal layman), and Robert Webber of Wheaton College (an Episcopal layman/theologian and authority on worship). Though I have read and reread their works, I cannot now always isolate which insights I first received where, nor with certainty which ideas are my own. In addition to these writers, there have been dozens of hours of conversation with friends—clerical and lay—around the world. I hope these kindred saints remember them with the same fondness that I do. As has often been noted, we stand tall because we stand on the shoulders of our teachers. My teachers in the crucial area of church and ministry, however, have been thinkers whom I have discovered on my own—by accident—and who, with one exception, were not members of my own denomination.

2

Who Are We?
A Functional Theology of the Church

Robert Webber reminds us of the story of Jane Doe, a middle-aged woman who in 1980 appeared in Florida, stricken with amnesia.[1] She couldn't remember who she was. She had a past, had a family and friends, had values and likes and dislikes, but she could remember none of it. Though she had an identity, she had lost it.

Can you imagine what that would be like? If you did not know who you were, you would not know how to act. Should you eat spinach? Should you go to work at the IBM office building? On Sunday, do you get up and go to church? If you have forgotten who you are, you are disoriented. You don't know what to do.

The same is true in the universal Church, or in your local church. Before we can know *what* to do, much less *how* to do it, we must recover our identity. If we are to rise from the ashes, we must learn again *who we are*.

What the Church Is Not

Before defining what the Church is, perhaps it will help to clear away some false ideas.

1. The Church is not a human organization based on common interests. Some people seem to think that the church is like the Rotary Club or the Ladies' Garden Society, that is, a group of people who are drawn together by some interest held in common. In this case everyone is interested in religion. All those interested in religious matters have gotten together and formed a "club." They have officers, regular meetings, and membership dues. This is a far cry from the biblical teaching.

2. The Church is not a social institution, like the government or the public schools. In our society, this idea goes, we have certain structures or institutions. So, the Church has officers, buildings and property, official leaders, schools to train those leaders, and a social function to fill. It is a false—or at least incomplete—idea.

3. The Church is not a corporation, a task-oriented business intent on "selling" something or "making a profit." This is, however, a common mind-set in many of our churches, particularly the very large ones. The procedures, methods of evaluation, and structures are often very similar to those of a corporation.

All these conceptions of what the Church is are faulty. Granted, the Church is made up of people, but it is not merely a human organization. Granted, the Church does have a role in society, but it is not a cultural institution. Granted, the Church must have some organization and a mission, but it is not a business.

What, then, is it?

Characteristics of the Church in the New Testament[2]

1. The Church is the community of the converted. Churches in the sacramental tradition would say that the Church is made of those who are baptized, but the position of evangelical churches is different. The Church, we would say, is made up of those who have consciously chosen to

follow Jesus as Lord. It is that group who have been converted and forgiven of their sin. Though no one in the Church claims to be perfect (well, few do, anyway), we do emphasize that we are those who belong to Christ and follow him. Evangelical churches welcome young children and inquirers, but the distinction must be made: the Church of Jesus is made of those who have made a conscious decision of the will to submit to Christ and follow him.

2. The Church is the community of the Holy Spirit, where the Spirit is active. In New Testament thought, the powers of the Age to Come have already become operative in Christ and in the Holy Spirit, present with us now. What distinguishes the Church from other religious bodies is that here, among the family of believers, God is at work in a supernatural way. God moves and changes people and events. This is what lifts Christianity above being simply dead doctrine and dry ethics.

The Book of Acts could well be called "The Acts of the Holy Spirit." Jesus sent the Spirit (1:5, 2:33). This Holy Spirit empowered the mission work (1:8, 4:31, 7:54, 8:29, 13:9) and guided the infant Church at its most crucial moments (4:8, 10:19, 13:2–4, 15:28, 16:6, 19:2, 21:4). Signs and wonders were done in the power of the Holy Spirit (2:43, 5:12), and a qualification for selection as one of the seven (deacons) was to be "full of the Spirit" (6:3). The Spirit produced the *koinonia,* the unity and fellowship, in the Church (2:43–5:11).

For Paul, having the Spirit at work within is the mark of belonging to Jesus (Gal. 3:1–6, Eph. 1:13, 14, Rom. 8:9), and it is the Spirit who produces Christian character (Gal. 5:22, 23), especially love (Rom. 5:5). The Spirit produces unity (Eph. 4:3) and serves as the down-payment for the life to come (Eph. 1:13, 14, Rom. 8:23).

Peter asserts that the Spirit converts and purifies believers (1 Peter 1:2, 12), and the author of Hebrews says that believers have "shared in the Holy Spirit" and have tasted "the powers of the coming age" (6:4, 5).

The Church is not a religious club, nor even a school for training in correct doctrine. It is the community where God is active.

3. In the New Testament, the Church is the community under Christ's lordship. In John's Gospel, the Church is not an institution centered around the Lord's Supper or church structures, but a community centered around the hearing and doing of Jesus' word: "You are my friends," Jesus said, "if you do what I command" (John 15:14). In Paul's work, the early Christian confession is prominent: "Jesus is LORD" (Rom. 10:9, Phil. 2:10). This ultimate allegiance to Christ supersedes all other allegiances, including family (Luke 14:26), country (20:20–25), and one's own life (9:23).

In the New Testament, the Church is the community of people who live under the authority, the Lordship, of Christ.

4. The Church is the community of people who are on mission. Because Israel had failed in its mission to be God's redemptive agent in the world, the task was passed to the new Israel, those who believe in Jesus as the Messiah (1 Peter 2:9, 10). Like Israel, the Church was not chosen by God simply to receive his blessing and grace; it has been given a task as well. The Church is to be the channel through which God works to save people.

Jesus gave to his Church the great Commission:

> . . . All authority in heaven and on earth has been given to me. Therefore go and make disciples of all nations, baptizing them in the name of the Father and of the Son and of the Holy Spirit, and teaching them to obey everything I have commanded you. And surely I will be with you always, to the very end of the age (Matt. 28:18–20).

Paul tells the Corinthians that

> God was reconciling the world to himself through Christ, not counting man's sins against them. And he has committed to us the message of reconciliation. We are therefore Christ's ambassadors, as though God were making his appeal through us (2 Cor. 5:19, 20).

The early Church understood itself to be a people on mission.

5. The Church is the community where church discipline is practiced. This was done in the apostolic period.

In Matthew 18:15–17, Jesus gives instructions on how to handle the problem of sin in the Church. First, the offended party should talk to the offender one to one. If there is no settling of the problem, the offended party should go and talk with the offender again, this time with one or two witnesses. If there is still no repentance, the matter is to be taken to the congregation. If the offender refuses to be guided by the counsel of the church, he is to be treated like "a pagan or a tax collector," that is, he is to be excluded.

Paul writes about the same issue to the church in Corinth. He orders the church (1 Cor. 5:4, 5) to expel an immoral member who is living with his stepmother. "When you are assembled in the name of our LORD Jesus," he advises, ". . . hand this man over to Satan, so that the sinful nature may be destroyed and his spirit saved on the day of the LORD." He goes on (v. 11) to remind them that they are not to associate with church members who are "immoral, or greedy, an idolater or a slanderer, a drunkard, or a swindler." "With such a man," he concludes, "do not even eat."

This is church discipline. This is the congregation helping its members to walk the straight path of obedience to Jesus. In the early churches, when one joined the fellowship, he submitted himself to the discipline of the group. If you went off the deep end, the church would lovingly try to correct you, just as parents discipline their children and just as James ordered (5:19, 20).

This is a foreign thought in most Western churches. We want a do-it-yourself religion, where there are few ethical demands—but it is not the biblical way.

6. The Church is the "ecclesia," the called-out of God. The New Testament word that we translate "church" is *ecclesia*. It comes from two Greek words that together mean

"the called-out ones." That is who we are. We are those people whom God has called out of sin and death and into new life in his Son.

We are not necessarily a structure or organization. We are a community of people who have been called out. "The Church" is not a building, a program, a denominational headquarters, or an organizational unit. It is *people*—those called out *by God*.

3

What Are We Doing Here?
The Five Tasks of the Church

When I was a boy growing up in Central Texas, my father was quite an avid hunter. He taught my brother and me about guns—how to be safe and how to shoot. An obvious truth emerged to me in all this: if you didn't aim at the right target, you would most likely miss it. To hit the target, you've got to know what the target is. Or, to put it another way, if you aim at nothing, you'll hit it every time.

For the Church to rise from the ashes, we must begin to fulfill our purpose. And before the Church can fulfill its purpose—and *know* if it is filling its purpose—we must determine what our target or purpose is: that is, we must identify our tasks. These tasks must then always be in the forefront of our thinking, planning, and evaluating of church life.

Others might list a different number of tasks, or call them by different names. Regardless these five issues are central, indispensable elements of the Church's identity and mission.

Further, all five tasks are essential if the Church, or your congregation, is to be complete and balanced. Christian friends in Australia have wondered whether each congregation is to perform all five tasks, or whether different congregations will emphasize one or another. My opinion is that though the gifts of a particular pastor may be in particular areas, the congregation should be active in all five areas. It is, after all, the pastor's role to *equip* the saints so that they may employ *their* gifts in the various ministries of the church (Eph. 4:11–13).

There is no "hierarchy" within the tasks, unless worship is first (and that would not be granted in most evangelical quarters). At any rate, here are the five tasks of the Church.

Worship

One of the Church's central tasks—perhaps the primary one—is that it be *a worshiping community.* We are the people of God, who gather weekly around our Savior to worship him.

It was at this point—worship—that my frustration with church life became acute. On more than one occasion I wanted to stand up at my seat in the choir loft, interrupt the service, and shout "What are we doing here?" I know that *I* didn't know what was supposed to happen, and I doubted that others did either. As I began to quietly ask the question, I became convinced that few Christians I knew had ever considered it. The deep feeling of emptiness and dissatisfaction convinced me that whatever was *supposed* to be happening when a large crowd of us gathered on Sunday, *wasn't.* And the few opinions that were offered on why we met together were (I intuitively sensed) far off-beam. It is, by the way, this deep, innate longing for proper, reverent worship that has led many evangelicals (by their own testimonies) into the liturgical churches: Episcopal, Lutheran, Presbyterian, Methodist, Roman Catholic.

The word *worship,* in both Hebrew and Greek, means "to bow down," "to prostrate oneself." When we gather together on Sunday morning, we gather "to bow down," to pause once a week and recognize our place, to realign our perspective. We "bow down" and acknowledge that he is God and we are not; we admit who he is and who we are.

The focus of worship then is *God,* not the preacher. We gather to praise God, to pray to him, perhaps to argue with him or complain to him. We speak to him, and we wait in silence for him to speak to us. It is not a jazzy pep rally; it is a bowing down. It does not have to be dull and boring, but it should be reverent. Indeed, the Book of Hebrews instructs us to "worship God acceptably, with reverence and awe" (12:28). And, the same verse tells us, the reason we worship is that we are thankful for what God has done.

Faulty Models of Worship

In the evangelical tradition, we have been served faulty models of worship.

1. We think of worship as entertainment. We are the "audience generation". Our church architecture even encourages it. The preacher and choir are up front, even on a raised stage platform. The place of worship is often called the "auditorium," the place where one goes to "audit", that is "listen." The chairs or pews are designed for maximum comfort, while we settle back to "watch the show," and they are arranged to focus attention on the stage. One or two people (the paid professionals up front) do all the speaking and acting.

Then if the show is "good," we leave church feeling good. If the service was fast-paced, with no breaks in the action (and televised or broadcast worship services makes it worse—the unpardonable sin of broadcasting is "dead air"); if the songs and mood were upbeat; and if the preacher really "nailed" the sermon, we say, "That was a good service." Whatever methods help the show—no matter how crass—are grabbed, be it spotlights up front, Hollywood look-at-what-I-can-do music, the latest trendy clothes, or handsome, virile preachers with lots of charisma—all is fair to beef up the entertainment value. And most television preachers, it goes without saying, are masters of these techniques.

One must admit that if entertainment is the goal, this approach is a good one. What we must ask, however, is whether entertainment *is* the goal of worship. And when we ask, we must answer *no;* the goal of worship is *to bow down,* not *to feel good* or *be entertained.*

You have perhaps heard Sören Kierkegaard's analogy of worship and the theater. In his day, he said, the Lutheranism of nineteenth-century Denmark followed the entertainment model. The congregation was the audience, the preacher was the actor, and the Holy Spirit was the prompter who whispered the lines to the actor (that is, the preacher). People came, sat, watched the show, and went home. Kierkegaard added that worship should be seen quite differently. God is to be the audience to whom we "play," the congregation are the actors, and the worship leaders are the prompters who whisper to the congregation how to bow down. The responsibility to worship, to bow down, pray, praise, and listen is *one's own,* not the preacher's. It does *help* if the choir sings on pitch and the sermon is good; but whether I approach God and bow down is up to *me,* the worshiper. This is a foreign idea, however, to our entertainment-minded congregations.

2. Another faulty model of worship in our midst is the *evangelistic approach.* This model flows from the revivalist heritage shared by most of American evangelicalism. The First Great Awakening swept the English colonies of the American Atlantic coast during and after the 1739-40 preaching tour of George Whitefield. Subsidiary awakenings continued in parts of America until a Second Great Awakening erupted in the years 1790-1830; its high point was 1800-1803 in Kentucky, where both Baptists and Methodists gained ten thousand new converts each. This revivalist tradition—very effective on the frontier—remained a central feature of church life in conservative Protestant groups, particularly among the Baptists and Methodists.

In the awakenings, the revival meeting was the favored evangelistic tool. People came to the meeting ("church service"), where they heard upbeat (for its day) music, compelling personal testimonies, and a vigorous, noisy proclamation of the gospel. The services were rowdy and the focus was the emotional "invitation" at the end, when people were called to make some kind of commitment to Christ. This technique led thousands into the kingdom and it is still widely used in many denominations. Many people today make significant commitments in such meetings; from rough polling, I conclude that one-third to one-half of the students in my seminary classes share this experience.

The question is *not* whether the revival meeting is a good evangelistic method, or whether it is outmoded, or whether it is too emotional and shallow. The question is whether the evangelistic, nineteenth-century, Southern revival meeting is to be the norm for the worship of God. And in many circles, it is.

Granted, there are occasionally lost people in a Sunday-worship service. Granted, the morning sermon should occasionally be evangelistic. But making every service, as one of my friends puts it, "a dog-and-pony show" to impress any lost people who happen to have stumbled in is a far cry from the Bible's call to "bow down" and offer praise and worship "with reverence and awe." Weekly worship is not a spectacular show to impress the lost; it is the family of faith gathered to worship its Lord. Nonbelievers are welcome to participate, but the service is not geared to woo them to become one of us. Evangelism is, in the main, to take place day-by-day in the homes, shops, and schools. But because we do not evangelize there, we have turned the worship of God into an evangelistic meeting.

3. A faulty model of worship that many follow is the *educational* pattern. In this approach the sanctuary becomes a lecture hall. The focus is the "teaching from the Word," that is, the sermon. Indeed preachers and laymen are often heard to refer to all that precedes the sermon as "the pre-

liminaries," which are to be dispensed with as quickly and painlessly as possible. When the sermon begins, out come the notebooks and pens. The preacher lectures on a passage of Scripture and the listeners dutifully take notes.

There is certainly to be in the worship service a well-prepared, biblical sermon, with good interpretation of the text and cogent application. And some Christians are at a place in their spiritual journey where they need to learn much, and taking notes perhaps will help. No one is objecting to the Word of God being taught (though much of what is taught as the Word of God is merely the opinions of the preacher—but that's another issue). What is objected to is turning the worship of God (with sermon) into an academic lecture. We do not gather on Sunday to hear a great lecture; we gather to worship our Risen Lord.

Barriers to Worship

These faulty models of worship reveal some barriers to our worship.

1. Our worship is *man-centered.* Rarely in Protestant worship is God the focus of attention. Nearly always attention is centered on *people*—the preacher, the choir, and me (how I feel, whether I agree with the preacher's ideas, what I'm "getting out of it"). We sit back to watch the one-man-band "do" the worship service. We do not focus on God, bowing down before him, talking to him, and listening for his word to us.

2. Related to this is a second barrier. Our worship is *rationalistic,* with little sense of mystery or awe. In conservative Protestantism we have little use for (indeed, suspicion of) color and symbols. This comes from the Calvinist Reformation's aversion to anything that smacked of Roman Catholicism. To see this comparison, contrast the aesthetic grandeur of Westminster Abbey in London with the white-washed walls of the Cathedral of Saint Pierre in Calvin's Geneva. Through Puritanism these views came to American Protestantism. We emphasize thought and word; we

eschew emotion. Witness our discomfort with Pentecostal worship forms. Christianity easily becomes a matter of right thought (theology) and right action (ethics). These are certainly crucial to Christian faith, but they are cold and dead without the life-giving warmth of the Holy Spirit's fire. The Christian faith is a supernatural, mysterious, awesome relationship with the Almighty God of the Universe, and it may not (contrary to our word-thought, rationalistic mind-set) be forced into a discipleship notebook. In our worship we speak and hear words and we evaluate the sermon's content, but we sense little mystery, for there is no mystery; everything is explainable in clear terms. We are word-oriented rationalists.

3. Our worship has *no personal spiritual* vitality. Hebrews 13:15 gives the key to acceptable worship: it is the natural, inevitable fruit of lips that confess his name. When a person daily walks with God, and daily relies on the living power of the Holy Spirit, he will not have to be coaxed to worship God. It will be the inevitable fruit of his faith. But when a church building is full of people who don't daily walk with God, people for whom God is only a concept (though a wholly orthodox one), or for whom Christianity is a rather tedious list of rules (though conscientiously obeyed), they will offer no worship to God. They will come and sit, expecting nothing and giving nothing. And at this point the church must resist structuring worship to entice or amuse such people. The enticing or amusing can take place elsewhere; worship is to be worship.

This entire discussion has—purposely—not even touched on musical styles or "free" worship versus "liturgical." Whatever styles lead a congregation to worship God should be employed, be it gospel music or Bach chorales. Musical tastes, it seems to me, are largely a matter of background and exposure, and are at any rate irrelevant to our main point: worship is to be a "bowing down" to God.

Fellowship (Love for the Brethren)

A second task of the Church, one which we must pursue if we are to be Christ's church, is *fellowship*. The word actually means "a sharing with someone in something." Paul uses it in the New Testament to describe the believer's sharing or participating in Christ, and for the mutual sharing of life among the believers. Christians are in spiritual communion with their Lord and thus with one another. It is more than mere friendship; it is a spiritual union in the same faith. This fellowship is to be expressed in how Christians relate to one another; it is shown in the love for the brethren.

It was this—the fellowship—that drew me to the Church and holds me in it. At age seven I made an intellectual commitment to Christ (the child's "yes, I believe in Jesus and I don't want to go to hell" type). I honestly don't know what the reality of my faith was. I had grown up attending Heights Baptist Church in Temple, Texas, with my family, and I continued to do so into my high school years. But between my brief childhood period of spiritual concern and my junior year in high school I had very little spiritual interest. I believed all the orthodoxy that I'd been taught, but there was little (or no) heartfelt following of Christ.

Then in the summer of my sixteenth year, before I began grade eleven, our small, dull, squabbling congregation called a youth minister. Gary Manning and his wife, Paulette, were all of twenty-two years old, brand-new graduates of Howard Payne College, a small Baptist school in Brownwood, Texas. To me they were mature, fun, "with-it." Gary began several activities for the small group of teenagers in our church, some fun activities and some serious ones. One of these was called "Dialogue" and was a weekly share group for high school and college students. I'm not sure why I first began to attend the activities, but I know what caught my attention. Not only were these people, led by Gary, talking about things that mattered (the intellectual side); I sensed the love for the brethren. It drew me inexorably into the group; it was almost palpable, intoxicating. I didn't know anyone's millennial view (or even that there were millennial views). I didn't know anyone's position on speaking in tongues (or even what it was). I didn't know who listened to rock music or occasionally drank a beer at home (though I would later be taught that these were *crucial* kingdom matters). All I knew was that there was a kinship, a "fellowship" here that I had never heard of and certainly never experienced.

Very quickly, our group of teenagers, who knew each other only very casually (perhaps not even speaking in the halls at school), became a close-knit, caring "family of faith." I suppose this first experience of Christian love, *koinonia*, fellowship, will continue to be the standard for me.

Even more important and influential was the undeniable effect of Gary's love and concern for *me*. For the first time in my life, I felt, someone beyond my family cared about me. I mattered to Gary Manning; he was concerned for me; he poured himself out for me. He didn't *have* to because, for example, he was a relative. He simply accepted me and cared about me. And the Holy Spirit, through the love for the brethren, did his work in my young life. By the end of that summer I had committed my life to Christian ministry because (as I remember telling a friend's mother) following Christ and knowing his people brought such joy that I wanted to spend my life helping others to know it. I was drawn to Christ and the Church, not because (as with Justin Martyr) Christianity provided the answers that torture an intellectual's mind, but because in the fellowship, the community of Christian people, I saw the love for the brethren.

I have felt it since in other places often enough for me to believe it can exist. It came to me in a group of my fellow university students; it came to me in a group of teenagers whom I served as youth minister; it came in a group of college students whose "spiritual leader" I was; it came in a group of businessmen who met each Wednesday morning at 6:00 to talk about their lives; it came in brief, one-week visits with Baptist congregations in Canada and Australia; and it comes with a group of seminary students who meet weekly.

Fellowship is notable by its presence in some groups of Christians; it is also notable for its absence in others. Nothing seems so fake and lifeless as "Christian groups" where there is no discernible love for the brethren. I have known churches without it and pastors to whom its practice is foreign.

When one reads the New Testament with all this in mind, one will be amazed at how often the Church is admonished to love one another. We are clearly commanded to love. In John 15:12 Jesus says "My command is this: Love each other as I have loved you." Five verses later (15:17) Jesus says, "This is my command: Love each other." And in John 13:34 Jesus says, "A new command I give you: Love one another. As I have loved you, so you must love one another."

Near the end of the first century the aged apostle John echoed his master's words:

> We know that we have passed from death to life, because we love our brothers. Anyone who does not love remains in death. Anyone who hates his brother is a murderer, and you know that no murderer has eternal life in him. This is how we know what love is: Jesus Christ laid down his life for us. And we ought to lay down our lives for our brothers. If anyone has material possessions and sees his brother in need but has no pity on him, how can the love of God be in him? Dear children, let us not love with words or tongue, but with actions and in truth (1 John 3:14–18).

The apostle Paul, in the famous love chapter (1 Cor. 13) agrees that love is more important than eloquent speech and tongues (v. 1), the gifts of inspired preaching, spiritual insight and knowledge, great faith (v. 2), or even of commitment that is willing to give all one has, even one's life, for Christ (v. 3). To have all those gifts and qualities but to not love, God's Word says, is to miss the point.

Further, love for the brethren is the proof to us that we are God's children (1 John 3:14), and it is the evidence to the pagan world that we are Christians. Jesus says, "All men will know that you are my disciples *if you love one another*" (John 13:35, italics added). The world will not know know that we are Christ's because we beat them over the head with our Bibles or because we are superficially pious. They will know because of the unique quality of caring that exists in our midst.

Several times, in group settings, I have asked Christians to briefly explain how they came into faith and active discipleship. Nearly without exception, as their stories unfold, the people mention someone who played a decisive role in their spiritual journey. And the story is always about a single person along the line who *cared* for them. They don't mention great sermons or famous books; they mention *people* who *cared*.

To be Christ's Church, we must love one another. We must create structures that enhance it, and eliminate structures that hinder it. And we must remember that *we* cannot love others like this. It is the Holy Spirit who produces this love in us (Gal. 5:22, 23). He will give it to us, if we will receive it.

> Therefore, as God's chosen people, holy and dearly loved, clothe yourselves with compassion, kindness, humility, gentleness, and patience. Bear with each other and forgive whatever grievances you may have against one another. Forgive as the LORD forgave you. And over all these virtues put on love, which binds them all together in perfect unity (Col. 3:12–14).

Evangelism

A third major task of the Church is *evangelism*. Our word *evangelism* comes from an older English word, "evangel," which comes from the Greek word *euangelion*. It means "a good report" or "good news" and was used, for example, when a messenger brought "good news" about the battle's progress to the commanding general. The Christian "good news," of course, is that we, who are rebellious sinners, can be forgiven and restored to God because Christ has died on the cross for us.

I was several years along in my spiritual journey and theological education before I clearly understood what "the gospel" was. It had gathered, in my denomination, church, and family, all kinds of cultural accretions, such as, no drinking, no dancing, no smoking, not wearing risqué clothes or swimsuits, always voting Democratic (or, nowadays, Republican), and being frugal.

In my early graduate school days I discovered a little book by C. H. Dodd entitled *The Apostolic Preaching and Its Developments.* It so intrigued me that I used it as a springboard for my master's thesis (one which few people, I suspect, have ever read). Dodd, writing in the thirties, tried to determine what it was that the apostles preached about. In the twenty to thirty years between the Lord's death and the writing of the first New Testament books, as the apostles "went everywhere preaching the gospel," what did they *say?* What was the content of their sermons?

Dodd took the apostolic sermons recorded in the Book of Acts as reliable paradigms or models of the early preaching. Comparing them, he found six major points:

1. Jesus came from God (Old Testament prophecy foretold his coming).
2. You killed him (he died for men's sin).
3. God raised him up.
4. The Holy Spirit is Christ present in the Church now.
5. He will come again.
6. Therefore, repent and believe the gospel.[1]

This, then, was the apostolic message; this is the gospel. Though Christian teaching must have much to say about ethical implications, about how we should live, about right and wrong, those things are not "the gospel." The Good News is that Christ came from God, died for our sins, rose, and will come again, and we, therefore, should turn from our sin and trust Christ for salvation. When we talk of evangelism, then, *this* is the message, and it is the Church's task to share it.

Why must we share this Good News? First of all, *we have the way to God.* Jesus' awesome claim in John 14:6 cannot be denied or explained away: "I am the way, and the truth, and the life. No one comes to the Father except through me." What he meant is very clear: *he* is the only way to God.

As we have all often heard, no other great religious leader made such a claim. Moses, Mohammed, Buddha, and others claimed to be spokesmen for God, to understand something about God, or to have insights that would point us to God. Jesus claimed to *be* God (John 1:1, 14; 10:30). It is a stupendous claim, and it is either right or wrong.

Jesus' tremendous claim has been a stumbling block to many people. "How," they ask, "can you Christians be so arrogant as to think that you are the only ones who are right—who know the way to God?" They continue, "If God were going to establish only one way, does it make sense that he would use a peasant in an obscure country on the back side of the Roman Empire in a far-distant century?"

Perhaps it does sound arrogant, but it need not be said arrogantly. We believe that Jesus was God in the flesh (John 1:1, 14) and that *he* said that he is the only way to God.

The real problem, it seems, is the problem of relativism. Modern people have difficulty accepting the idea of an absolute, that is, a truth that is always true, for all people, in all places. We prefer to believe that all values and teachings are relative, that is, that they may or may not be true, depending on who you are, when and where you live, and what your family and culture are like. Everything is, then, *relative* to one's situation; nothing is absolute.

From this position, the Christian point of view is arrogant and proud. These people argue that all religions are really the same, that they all lead to the same conclusion, and that all men of goodwill are going to arrive at the same destination.

But one needs only to study the religions of the world to see that *each* claims to have *the* truth, and that they teach different things. They obviously cannot all be equally true, all the same.

The Christian message then is that there is a correct way to see God and his relationship to man, and that way is through Jesus Christ. Though Christ may be a stone of stumbling to some, he is the foundation stone at the same time. Though Moses, Mohammed, and the Buddha may have some good insights and helpful teachings, we believe that in Jesus God has *acted* to meet and save us. Christ is unique. In him God has done a unique thing, something he has done nowhere else: He has acted to redeem us.

An international student from the Middle East, a Muslim, once said to me, "Here's how I think it works. When you die, God weighs all your good deeds and bad deeds, and if you have more good than bad, you make it to heaven." I responded, "We Christians believe that no one would ever have enough good deeds to be acceptable to God. That's why Jesus came to die in our place and pay for our sins. We come to God because Jesus has paid our debt." He answered, "Yes, I know that's what you Christians think." End of conversation.

If the student was right, then which religion you practice really does *not* matter; what matters is living a moral life. But if I was right, then it does make a difference, for only Christianity says that we cannot please God in ourselves. The New Testament gives the Good News, though, that we don't *have* to please God in ourselves. It tells us that Jesus has died to make us right with God. *This is the gospel.*

The people you know may not care to know God. But if they are to ever know him, they must come to him through his Son, Jesus the Christ. We must evangelize because Jesus is the only way to God.

The second reason that the Church must share the gospel is because *people need Christ, both now and for eternity.*

Life without Christ, without being forgiven and related again to God, will be empty and unhappy. People are made by God for relationship with him. We have physical, intellectual, emotional, *and spiritual* dimensions to our existence. But we have all rebelled against God and severed the relationship with him. With the spiritual element truncated, we live impoverished lives. The great Father of the Church, Augustine, said in *The Confessions,* a prayer to God, "You have made us for yourself, and our heart is restless until it rests in you."

I know a middle-aged man who knows the truth of Christ, but who will not give over to it. He refuses to bow the knee to Christ and accept forgiveness. My friend is nearly forty years old, and in the last twenty years—the years of his adulthood—nearly everything he has touched has fallen apart. He cannot understand what is wrong, why he is so unhappy, why he cannot find "the key" to make sense of life. I do not want to oversimplify life. There are many reasons why a person's existence is miserable. But the crucial, foundational element is this: one's relationship to God. Though Christian believers may be unhappy and have to struggle to overcome painful pasts, the person who is far from Christ has no chance at fulfillment and happiness; the primal, elemental issue of life, one's relationship to his Creator, has not been made right. People need Christ now, in this life.

But people need Christ for another reason, and that is that life will continue for eternity.

The Bible is very clear that life continues after the moment of physical death. And the Bible teaches that one's eternal state (blessedness or punishment) will be determined by whether one in this life was still rebellious against

God or had "come home" to his Maker. These eternal destinies are called in Scripture "heaven" and "hell."

When Jesus cast about for a figure of speech to describe the horror of life in eternity without God, he fell upon the word translated into Greek as *gehenna* ("hell"). It was a very graphic word, for it referred to the Valley of Hinnom outside Jerusalem. It was the garbage dump for the city. There were mountains of refuse, and fires were kept burning to consume the rubbish. The bodies of criminals were thrown on top of the heap, and the stench of the place was horrendous. For a good Jew, fastidious in keeping the ceremonial purity of the Jewish Law, there could be no more repulsive, filthy, macabre place than the Valley of Hinnom. And that, Jesus said, is a good metaphor for what eternity apart from God will be like. We, the Church, must evangelize, for people need Christ both now and for eternity.

The third reason why the Church must share the gospel is because *Christ has given to us the ministry of reconciliation.*

In 2 Corinthians 5:19 is the heart of the gospel message: "God was reconciling the world to himself in Christ, not counting men's sins against them. . . ." It is a great report! God was reconciling us to himself in Christ! But the next verses carry the responsibility that goes with the privilege.

> . . . and he has committed to us the message of reconciliation. We are therefore Christ's ambassadors, as though God were making his appeal through us. We implore you on Christ's behalf: Be reconciled to God (vv. 18–20).

The ambassador of a king was sent in the king's authority, to deliver the king's message. And we, the Church, are Christ's ambassadors. He calls all men to repent and believe, and he makes his appeal *through us.* We must evangelize, because Christ has given to his Church the message of reconciliation.

Though most Christians would agree that we *are* to share the gospel, most would also agree that few *do* it. There are some reasons for this.

1. *Some Christians seem unsure whether people are really lost.* We all know non-Christians who are fine people, moral, and loving. They don't fit the old mold of "filthy, rotten sinners bound for hell." In fact, they seem to have as good or better a handle on life than we do. And, for some Christians, as theology weakens, so does the urgency of evangelism and the sense of lostness of people.

We who are the Church must get a new grip on the truth that people apart from Christ, however nice they may be, are lost and destined for eternal separation from God. People really are lost.

2. *We are timid about evangelism because we have seen perversions of it.* Preachers who are more concerned about "numbers" than about people are not infrequent, and many of us see right through their veneer of piety. Sensitive Christians are hurt by manipulative methods that prey on people's psychological needs, and they find themselves wanting to keep away from such techniques (1 Thess. 2:3–6). But we must be careful not to throw the baby out with the bath water. Simply because we abhor underhanded methods of evangelism does not mean that we should not evangelize at all.

3. Many Christians are timid about witnessing because *unrealistic, unreachable models are held up before us.* We are taught that Paul charged around the Mediterranean world witnessing nonstop from sunup to sundown. This is the way "really dedicated" Christians will witness. We sense that this is unrealistic. Perhaps we remember that Paul also earned his living in a "secular" job, which cut into his available time for nonstop evangelizing.

But still we hear it: "It's all right to be a lawyer [or teacher, salesman, bricklayer, whatever] as long as you are a witness to those in your field." Notice the implication. It's not all right to be a lawyer or whatever. It's only all right to be a witnessing machine who makes a living in some job. We have been told that our only reason for existence is to be witnesses. And for many that wears thin. It is patently

simplistic. Because we cannot accept this approach to witnessing, we do not witness at all, which is worse.

We must take seriously the Bible's teachings on this matter. If we have experienced salvation in Christ, then we can
"witness to" or "testify" about what we have seen, as a
witness in a courtroom testifies only about what he or she
has actually seen or heard. In this sense, all Christians are
"witnesses." But some, the Bible teaches (Eph. 4:11), have
from God a special gift of evangelism, of leading people to
faith in Christ.

I do not have this gift, but I have seen it at work in those
who do have it. On one occasion I went visiting with a
fellow pastor who manifests this gift. Neither of us knew
the young couple we called on. After less than a minute of
chatting with them about their jobs, my friend (in my es-
timation) "barged" into the gospel, asking the husband if
he knew with certainty that he would go to heaven if he
died (the standard Evangelism Explosion question). I was
shocked. I expected the husband to become irate and throw
us out of the house. Had I taken that approach, it would
have been very unnatural and forced, and I am certain that
the husband would have been offended. But to my surprise
the husband was immediately drawn into a deep, medita-
tive silence. "No, I'm not certain," he said. My friend then
explained the gospel, and though the man did not then
decide to follow Christ, he was considering it and he knew
what it meant to be a Christian. My friend has the gift of
evangelism, which is I think not only the boldness to speak
of Christ, but the spirit that does so naturally and without
offense.

What we have done in the Church, however, is to hold
up this kind of person as the model for all believers. We
have not taken seriously the idea of the diverse gifts of the
Holy Spirit.

I rejoice that some have this unusual ability to win the
lost to Christ. I do not rejoice, however, that other Christians are made to feel guilty because they do not have it.

Those who do have it should be set free from other church jobs (for which they are probably not gifted) to concentrate on evangelism. And how many in a congregation will have this gift? No one, of course, knows, but evangelism expert Peter Wagner suggests perhaps 10 percent will have it.[2] We must encourage and activate the 10 percent who are evangelists, and remember that we *all* are witnesses. But we must not refrain from evangelizing because an unrealistic model, one which most of us are not gifted to match, is held before us.

4. The Church is timid about evangelizing because *we are afraid of letting someone know what is important to us and risking rejection.* Our self-esteem is on the line. No one likes rejection (in spite of the story about the church member who enjoyed rejection so much that he put quarters into empty Coke machines so he would get nothing back). Rather than run the risk of having someone fling back in our face what we hold dear, we do not offer it at all. Though much could be said about this subject, it will have to wait until later.

Nurturing (Spiritual Growth)

The fourth task of the Church is *nurturing believers.* This could be called "discipleship" or "spiritual growth" or "Christian education."

In our church family there is a beautiful little one-year-old girl. Though she does not yet much appreciate my preaching (or maybe she does—I have put her to sleep regularly), little Amanda is precious to me. She is so small and in so many ways helpless. For her to grow and become a mature part of the human family, she must be nurtured. Not only food and water must be provided, but also the love and support that will enable her to become a mature, confident person.

In the Christian faith and life, too, people must be nurtured. The Bible speaks of coming into faith as being "born

again," and we often call recent converts "babes in Christ."
The Book of Hebrews (6:1) urges us to "go on to maturity",
and Paul reminded the Ephesians (4:13, 14) that God gave
spiritual leaders to the Church to nurture people:

> until we all reach unity in the faith and in the knowledge of the
> Son of God and become mature, attaining to the whole measure
> of the fullness of Christ. Then we will no longer be infants, tossed
> back and forth by the waves. . . .

I count myself fortunate that I have been nurtured in the
faith; other Christians, who saw my spiritual helplessness,
did not let me starve.

I gave my life to Christ when I was seven years old. I
understood little of the Bible or theology, but I did sense
some nudging toward God. In my earliest years it was my
parents who nurtured me. They took us to church, taught
us to acknowledge God, and emphasized that the Bible was
true and should be believed and practiced.

At age sixteen, I experienced a genuine encounter with
Christ. Whether this was conversion or a more mature (that
is, adolescent) appropriation of my faith, I don't know.
What I do know is that God used a *person* to reawaken
faith and commitment, and to nurture that faith.

Earlier in this chapter, while discussing love for the
brethren, I have told of a young youth minister, Gary Manning, and his profound impact on me during my teenage
years. Love for the brethren and nurturing begin to over-
lap, for it is in the love for the brethren that nurturing takes
place. That Gary served in our congregation when he did
was one of God's graces to me; many young people in our
churches are not nurtured. They "fall through the cracks."
We evangelicals, as a friend has pointed out, are good re-
cruiters (evangelists) but poor nurturers. This, thank God,
was not my fate.

But *how* do we nurture Christians so that they "reach
maturity"? *Are* we nurturing well now, or are we far off
beam? How *do* we "teach Christianity"? This is terribly

important; as Wayne Rood says, "In nurturing Christians, teaching is a soul-making thing to do."[3]

Perhaps first we should decide what nurturing *is not.*

Nurturing (or discipleship or Christian education) is not a rationalistic, content-centered lecture. I hope that my experience is not a common one, but I have never been in an adult Sunday-school class that was much else. People who know one another only superficially sit together in a room at the church. The "teacher" gives a monologic lecture, comprised usually of shallow, pious platitudes (for example, "if you don't use your gifts, you lose them"); no one shares anything about their *lives* (because they don't know each other well enough to ever get really honest and personal); pat answers are exchanged, and we call it "Christian education."

This simplistic, theoretical chat about religious things ("Do you believe that God can answer prayer?" "Oh, sure, I've always believed that.") is often neither quality Bible teaching nor honest grappling with the spiritual life. It constricts itself to the level of a petty moralism, a superficial transfer of information, a mouthing of true but lifeless concepts. When it is over, the people often know no more about what God says to us in the Bible (we would call that "too academic") and are not encouraged and strengthened in their Christian life ("that is too personal"). They have not learned (in a cognitive, content-oriented sense) much of importance, and they have not grown (in an emotional, spiritual sense). An hour has been spent, some light fellowship has occurred, and a religious theme has been discussed. That is not the same as nurturing.

In nurturing, people *do* need to learn content. New converts know very little about Christianity, and they need to learn about it. Correct doctrine and correct morality are crucial. I'm not suggesting that they don't matter. I'm suggesting that we're doing a poor job of teaching it and a poor job of shaping the new Christians whom God gives to our care.

Christians—particularly young Christians or recent converts—need grounding in the basic content of the Christian
faith. Some churches, like the Church of the Savior in
Washington, D.C., hold introductory classes that really get
into serious content.[4] We must do a better job of this. I
doubt that many lay people in our churches have a coherent
overview of the Old and New Testaments, much less Church
history, biblical theology, Christian ethics, or any system-
atic theology. This is, again, a result of our scattershot approach to Bible study, with its emphasis on moralizing
from the text. Christians need to know the Christian world-
view of creation, fall, redemption, eschatology. These matters of content are simply the basics for a fruitful Christian
life. Biblical and theological illiteracy are epidemic in the
churches.

Part of the problem is that in the local church we have
adopted secular educational models. The emphasis is on
following the denomination's age-grading scheme, following the quarterly, and getting out on time. I have a good
friend who teaches in the School of Religious Education in
the seminary where I also teach. He says (in not so many
words) that secular models of education are good, if they
are used well. When done properly, standard educational
techniques will take students from the cognitive (intellectual) to the affective (emotional) domain; teaching should
not be simply an intellectual lecture or discussion. I accept
what he says. I also think that he agrees that "Christian
education" rarely reaches this lofty goal. Here, as everywhere else in church life, we face the results of what Gene
Getz calls "creeping institutionalism," in which external
forms, patterns, and "just doing it" become more important than people.[5]

What must happen in nurturing is that we must *form*
Christians, not only (or primarily) *educate* Christians.

Christian nurturing is far *more* than cognitive transfer
of information, (for example, the kingdoms split in 922 B.C.,

Israel fell in 722 B.C., and Judah fell in 587 B.C.) It is the *forming* of disciples, not just the *educating* of disciples.

To do this—to shape and form people into authentic disciples of Christ—we must create an alternative society, a Christian one, in which people can learn to live like Christ. Conversion should be an exit out of culture, at least from the culture's shaping of our values. Christians are to be different from the world, not only in the obvious moral areas (sexuality, business, and so forth), but in the more basic area of values. We who are in the body of Christ must nurture less mature Christians to shed their pagan values and incorporate into their lives the values of Christ.

This is crucial, because people must live in some culture, and it is from one's culture that values are transmitted and encouragement comes to remain faithful to those values. That is why I meet each week with a group of fellow Christians. We remind each other of the ideal (Christ's teachings about how we should live) and encourage and support each other in trying to live that way. We nurture each other to become more and more like Christ and less and less pagan.

I am not arguing that Christians are to become "weird," "sectarian" people. Life is to be lived and enjoyed, and God wishes us to be happy. I am arguing, though, that if the pagan society (or any of its subcultures) shape our values, we are not following Christ. I may (without sin) go to football games and enjoy a movie, but I pray that I base my life on what God says is important (God, loving my family, being moral) and not what the world says is important (BMWs, corner offices).

My little three-year-old daughter goes to ballet class. After the first day, she cried and told her mom that she didn't like it. Mom assured her that each time she went the steps would get easier. They did. Now Meredith wouldn't miss dance class, and by the way (proud father that I am) I think she does very well.

This brings us to the old saying "Christianity is caught, not taught." People "catch" living like Christ by being around others who live like Christ. Disciple making, like ballet, comes in the master-apprentice relationship. William Willimon notes:

> Christian development is best understood, not as the ordered progression through various "stages of faith" (as in the work of James Fowler) or as instantaneous, momentous conversion (as in American evangelicalism) or as articulate self-expression (as in American liberalism), but rather as apprenticeship in the art of discipleship. Being Christian is more like learning to paint or to dance than it is like having a personal experience, or finding out something about oneself. It takes time, skill, and the wise guidance of a mentor. Discipleship implies discipline—forming one's life in congruence with the desires and directives of the Master.[6]

If Willimon is right, and I think that in the main he is, then the church must see itself as the body which nourishes people into an alternative (but not pagan) society and life.

This will not happen in large groups. People can worship in large groups of one hundred or one thousand or ten thousand, but Christians are formed in small groups where they are known and know others—where they are encouraged and supported—and where the master-apprentice model is real. It is in a small group that love is built, sin is faced, and strength comes. Here the disciplines of the spiritual life (prayer, Bible reading, and so forth) become habits of the new life.

Historically, this has always been the case. The early New Testament congregations were small groups, meeting in homes. There were no megachurches, with multimillion-dollar physical plants. Christians knew each other face-to-face. And in the great periods of renewal in the Church's history, the recovery of small groups is paramount. In the Wesleyan revival in England, in Pietism in eighteenth-century Germany, and in the Great Awakening in America, maturity came as Christians met together in small groups to nurture and be nurtured.

And it is happening today. The Methodists are reemphasizing their Wesleyan roots of small groups for nurture. The Roman Catholics have a parish renewal program called Renew, and Southern Baptists have a new discipleship program called MasterLife.[7] These programs center around small groups of Christians meeting together and practicing the spiritual disciplines, guided by a mature mentor. And as a Southern Baptist minister observed to me, "It isn't the program," for example, the notebook or the weekly assignments, that makes the idea work. It is the body of Christ, through which the Spirit shapes us into Christian people.

Service (Helping People)

A friend of mine has finally left a very large, very prominent, very affluent evangelical church in our city. It came over the church's refusal to be a servant church. With an annual budget near $3.5 million, the church recently provided in its budget two thousand dollars for "benevolence," that is, ministry to the needy. At the business meeting where this budget was to be approved, my friend's wife made a plea for more money for the poor. The moderator spurned her cry. The next year, the church reduced the "benevolence" budget to one thousand dollars, while it designated twenty-five thousand dollars for the church's seventy-fifth anniversary celebration. When my friend's wife again made an impassioned plea for more resources for the needy, the moderator of the business meeting squelched her dissent with "I'm sure the anniversary celebration will be one that you'll be proud of." To my friend and his family, the church was more concerned about itself, its luxuries, and its own organizational growth than it was about servanthood. So they left.

Perhaps nothing in the Bible is clearer than that Christ's people—his Church—are to be a servant people.

Jesus himself was the Suffering Servant Messiah. The Servant Songs of Isaiah 42–53 foretold a Messiah who would *not* drive out Israel's enemies, *not* lead Israel to economic greatness, and *not* "win" in any earthly sense. He would, on the contrary, suffer, be abused, despised, rejected, and would finally die. This Messiah would not be a powerful king like David; he would be a lowly servant, humiliated, who would be killed. Jesus lived that role.

He also taught it. I have always been especially fascinated by a story in the Gospels (Mark 10:35–45 and parallels). In it, Jesus was nearing the end of his ministry. With his disciples, he was on the road to Jerusalem for the feast of Passover. Finally, his disciples thought, Jesus would launch the revolution. Jerusalem would be packed with thousands of pilgrims from throughout the Mediterranean world. The confrontation between Jesus and the Jewish authorities had been brewing. Now, they felt sure, Jesus would make his move to become the new Jewish king, raise an army, and drive out the Romans.

So, James and John sidled up to Jesus on the road and asked that when he established his kingdom they be allowed to sit on his right and left hands. That is, they wanted the positions of power, prestige, and prominence. They wanted to be Secretary of State and Secretary of Defense in his new cabinet.

When the other disciples heard what James and John had asked, they became furious (because, I've always thought, James and John had beaten them to it). Here were the twelve disciples, who had been with Jesus for three years, squabbling about who would get the "big shot" positions. Jesus had to sit them down and straighten them out.

Among the pagans—those who don't know God—he told them, greatness is measured in terms of authority and power. But, he continued, it is not to be so among you. If you want to be great in the kingdom of God, you must be the servant of all. *Greatness in the kingdom of God is measured in the opposite way from the world's standard.* In the pagan society, no one wants to hold the lowly position of a servant; but Jesus said that one's servanthood is the measure of one's greatness in God's kingdom. He turned the values of the world upside down. To be Christ's people, we must be the lowly servants of others. Other passages in the New Testament make this point indisputable (Phil. 2:5–11, John 13:1–17).

This has been the weakest and slowest part of my Christian training and experience. As a child I was evangelized. Then, and later as a teenager, I was taught Bible stories. I was loved. I worshiped (after a fashion). But I was rarely taught or shown that as a Christian, my basic manner of life was to be that of a servant.

This came, I suppose, from a number of sources. One is that the church of my youth was a blue-collar congregation. People were very concerned with upward social mobility. That *seems* to clash with servanthood; perhaps it needn't. Second, it seems to me as I remember that the version of Christianity propounded and taught was a rather superficial "get saved, avoid gross moral sins, and witness" type. I don't want to be uncharitable, and I realize that perhaps my immaturity caused me to miss the deeper level of teaching; but I don't think so. To analyze one's cultural values, critique them in light of the gospel, and radically redirect one's life requires a certain level of analytical ability and perhaps leisure. At any rate, my opinion is that ordinary, run-of-the-mill, middle-class American Christianity rarely emphasizes servanthood, for it rarely questions its cultural values.

To be the Church of Jesus, however, we must emphasize *servanthood*. Authentic discipleship moves us to serve others. If our Christian faith does not cause us to love others, be concerned for them and help them, then it is suspect, if not bogus. James said that true religion involves moral purity *and* helping the needy (1:27), and Jesus warned that, at the last judgment, the reality of our faith will be measured by what we have *done* to help the needy (Matt. 25:31–46). John tells us that if we do not help those in need, we have no ground for claiming that we know God and have his love (1 John 3:14–18).

My heart is warmed when I see or hear about Christians donating money so that a poor child in town can have a necessary surgery, or when I hear of a woman in the church buying tennis shoes for two children in a poor family as the new school year begins. Offerings for world hunger relief cause the angels to sing. We must *be* servants and *do* servanthood.

But we don't—not much anyway—and usually not without a struggle. Why do we resist servanthood?

One reason sometimes heard is that helping people is worse than just "social ministry"; it is "that liberal-social-gospel stuff." I doubt that people who say this have ever read Walter Rauschenbusch and thus know anything about the social-gospel emphasis. And if they question whether Christians are to help those in need, I doubt if they have carefully read the Bible.

It must be granted, however, that we often find the social ministry emphasis in denominations that are, from an evangelical's point of view, quite liberal in theology. A characteristic of the mainline denominations in America since 1950, for example, has been a preoccupation with social concerns. Those denominations have also (generally) adopted a rather liberal theological stance. Since we see the two (liberal theology and social ministry) together in these denominations, we assume that they are corollaries. But we are wrong. Perhaps some liberal groups, with little confidence in the traditional evangelistic message and method, are left only with "trying to make the world a better place," that is, social ministry. That does not mean, however, that helping the needy is "liberal," that providing food, agricultural training, or medical care to Third World people is "liberal," or that being concerned about the homeless and hungry in your own town is "unspiritual" or "liberal." It is not "liberal"; it is *Christian,* and we are commanded by our Lord to be involved in it.

Christians who say that they are committed to the Bible's authority should stop arguing about how much they believe the Bible and start *doing* what it says! And when we do, we will find ourselves involved in helping the needy—in servanthood. Evangelism and servanthood are not options between which the church may choose; *both* are commanded. The excuse for neglecting servanthood because "it is liberal" will not hold water.

A second reason that many Christians are not servants is more honest: it is that we just don't want to be servants.

We live today in a "winner" society. We value the winners, whether it be in sports, business, or wars. Does anyone remember who came in third place in the NFL West last year? No. We don't *care* who came in third; we want to know who won the Super Bowl. The American Dream is success, climbing to the top of the ladder, making it, winning. We hear it all the time. We are bombarded with it on television and in movies—but nobody wants to be a servant.

In most metro areas, on most weekends, you could go to a conference in some church where a person (for a fee) will tell you how God wants you to be rich. (Of course, you see how *he's* getting rich.) "Just believe God for the BMW and it's yours," we're told. We have allowed the dominant values of American life—success and materialism—to enter the Church. In my opinion, the whole "gospel of wealth and success" package is both heresy and blasphemy, and God will judge the purveyors of it. But a recent vice-president of the Southern Baptist Convention has been roundly applauded for his book *See You at the Top.* The implication is clear: we want to be winners and want to be around winners. If you're going to see me, you'll have to be at the top.[8]

This obsession with success, money, and power is the American Dream carried to its logical conclusion. It is middle-class Americanism, pure and simple. It is more motivated by greed, selfishness, and pride than by Christ. And in the churches, we have bought it. We want to be "at the top," not "at the bottom." We will come to church services in our thirty-thousand-dollar automobiles, and we'll come to church aerobic classes in our eighty-five-dollar jogging suits. But we will be "at the top." And we don't want anyone to remind us that children are starving around the world and that in our towns there are people who *can't* jog, much less "make it to the top." We coat our Americanism with a thin veneer of Christianity in an attempt to make it more palatable, but God will not have it. Let's call this version of the American Dream what it is: selfishness, self-centeredness, and sin. This "reason" for not being a servant will not wash either.

To be a servant in modern-day America (or Canada, Australia, or Europe) will call for a radical reappraisal of our values and a radical readjustment of our lifestyles. We will become a "peculiar" people in a world consumed with winning. We will be out of step with the mass of people, particularly our upwardly/socially-mobile peer group. And many of us will not have the strength to do it. When we acquiesce to the culture's values and desire winning more than serving, let us be honest and stop calling ourselves faithful. For we are not.[7]

These, then, are the five tasks of the Church. To be the faithful Church of Jesus Christ, we must be involved in all of them. To fail to do so is to remain in the ashes—dead—with the form of religion but without its power.

4

Principles that Shape Church Life
How to Plan, Program, and Evaluate Your Church

M arian Alder is an old man. He lives in Poland, and is president of the Lublin Jewish Social-Cultural Association. He does not believe in God. As a youth he became a Communist, was arrested in pre-World War II Poland, and spent three years in prison. He was recently asked by a visitor, "What do you think of Communism now?" "You know," he replied, "it is a beautiful idea. Noble. But it depends on who carries it out."[1]

The same could be said about church life. The idea of a group of people, deeply committed to Christ, living out their discipleship together is a beautiful, noble idea. But it depends on who carries it out. Or, we could say, it depends on *how* it is carried out.

Church life should not be a series of knee-jerk, emotional responses to situations. It should be guided by broad, general principles.

We are following the pattern that will bring us up from the ashes into new life. We have already defined *who* we are as the Church. We have discussed what we are *to do* as the Church. We can now investigate *how* to live out Christ's life, that is, we can enunciate principles to guide us in our planning, programming, and evaluation. These principles fall into four general categories (*Basics, People, Programming, Structure and Function*) and twenty-two specific considerations.

The Basics

1. We must be obedient to Christ.

If we dare to call ourselves and our churches "Christian," then a fundamental principle must be that, whatever it costs or however we may feel about a situation, we will be obedient to Christ.

In the evangelical tradition we have emphasized this, the commitment side of Christianity. Most of our worship services culminate in an invitation to commitment. Our smug criticism of other denominations (rather than being theological) is usually that "those people aren't really committed." In our circles, the medieval monastics have been replaced as the models of commitment and devotion by missionaries: "*Those* people are really serious."

I suppose it is a good thing that we so often mention and evaluate commitment (though Robert Webber warns us against church services becoming a celebration of our commitment rather than of Christ). I do sometimes grow weary of being harangued almost weekly to be more committed, though on the other hand I sometimes need to hear it.

But regardless of our feelings about it, *obedience to Christ* is both the beginning and the bottom line of Christian life. It is not *optional,* and there are no sabbaticals granted. If we are to follow Christ, then we must deny ourselves, take up our crosses daily, and *follow* him (Luke 9:23). Jesus said that we are his friends *if* we do what he commands (John 15:14).

This is basically a matter of attitude or intention. We

determine that—come what may—we will be obedient to the Lord.

In the city where I work there is a university, Texas Christian University. In the early 1980s, a new head football coach, Jim Wacker, took over the football program. A Christian man with a vibrant personality, he revitalized the program at TCU within a couple of years. From being the Southwest Conference doormat, TCU became a contender for the conference championship. Then, at the beginning of the 1985 season, Coach Wacker learned that several starters on his team, including a Heisman Trophy-candidate running back, had been illegally recruited and had accepted money to come to TCU. Wacker himself called in the NCAA investigators and put the players off the team. In the next two seasons, TCU again became the doormat of the Conference. The great comeback was lost. The momentum TCU had achieved was gone. Coach Wacker was asked at a civic club luncheon if it had not been a very difficult decision to reveal the illegalities and call in the NCAA. He replied, "No, it was not a difficult decision. I made that decision years ago." He had years before decided that his athletic programs would be run according to the rules, even if it were difficult.

This is what the Church, what *your* church, must decide. We must determine to be obedient to Christ, period. We cannot debate being obedient in light of every new situation. We cannot first calculate how it will "hurt" us or our congregation, then decide about obedience. The first principle must already be set: we *will* be obedient to Christ. If this is not firmly established, set in concrete, then we can forget all the rest.

2. We must depend on the leadership and power of the Holy Spirit.

A second crucial principle concerns the source of direction and power in the Church's life, and that source is the Holy Spirit.

The Scriptures teach that Christians are the temple of the

Holy Spirit (1 Cor. 6:19) and that Jesus has given the Holy
Spirit to the Church to guide and lead it (John 14:16–18,
26). The Spirit is the Life-giver and we are admonished to
stop quenching the Spirit's fire (1 Thess. 5:19).

There is a lot of undergrowth around the Bible's teaching
about the Spirit; perhaps we could make it very simple by
saying that the Holy Spirit is God present now within us
individually and together as the Church. To know the life
and power of God, we must know the life and power of the
Holy Spirit. Those who are not of a Pentecostal or charismatic bent should not be frightened away from this idea.

To be a Christian then is to live in the power of the Holy
Spirit, and to be the Church is for a body of Christ's people
to live in the reality and power of God present with us
now. Otherwise the Church is merely another human
institution.

Perhaps you have heard the old saying that the Holy
Spirit could leave most churches and no one would notice
it for a year. Let's hope that's not true, but the saying does
point to the danger of institutionalism. It is easy (and some
would say necessary for large congregations) to fall into
corporate-business patterns in church life. The local church,
as a visible organization, is in some ways like a business:
there are people, employees, buildings, and money to be
managed. It becomes difficult to operate an organization
of several dozen (or several hundred or several thousand)
people without "getting organized," that is, setting up
channels, procedures, methods, and processes.

Unless we are careful, however, the church can become
simply an institution, an organization, a structure. Granted,
it is a *religious* organization, dealing with *religious* concepts
and products, but it is a bureaucratic structure nonetheless.
It is easy for us to lose the Holy Spirit's voice, simply to
carry on with our traditional methods. To be quite honest,
most evangelical groups can gather a congregation, build
a building, staff the church's ministries, and meet a budget
merely with the use of human methodology and tech-

niques. Most "church activity" can be accomplished and explained in merely human terms. There is little supernatural life. To carry on the "business as usual" of the average church, the Spirit is not necessary.

But that is exactly the point: is the local church's task to carry on "business as usual"? Are we really being the Church (body of Christ) when we simply gather groups, build buildings, and staff the Sunday school? The answer, of course, is *no*.

The Church is to be the presence of Christ in the world. It is in the body of the Church that the power and reality of God are seen and experienced. The powers of the Age to Come are present in our midst now, and we experience a foretaste of heaven in the Church. The Christian life, then, and the Church's life, is to be an experience of the supernatural, of God, here and now. The local church can be a human institution, carrying on religious activities, or it can be the arena of God's presence with us, where God speaks and works and changes us.

We must learn to depend on the Spirit to lead us and to do his work through us. Though a pastor should study during the week to prepare his sermon, there is a world of difference between his doing it as if he were preparing a religious talk and his asking and trusting the Spirit to lead and help him. Committees may meet and plan the church's work, but they can do it depending on the Spirit to guide or not. It sounds trite because we have heard it so many times, but it remains true: the Church is to be the group through whom God's presence and power flows. In our churches we must determine to seek and follow the Spirit's leadership and to depend on his power.

3. To follow the Holy Spirit in faith will sometimes appear foolish or risky.

The New Testament, particularly the Book of Acts, is the book of the Holy Spirit. It tells of people hearing and obeying the Spirit, and sometimes what the Spirit told them to do seemed foolish, risky, untraditional, or downright wrong.

The Spirit told Philip to leave a thriving revival movement in Samaria and go south, where he met a eunuch from Ethiopia (Acts 8:4–40). It seems a poor use of opportunity to leave a place where one is being used by God in a mighty way and go somewhere else; but that's what the Spirit told Philip to do. The Spirit, in a dream, told Peter that the Gentile Cornelius *was* acceptable to God, which seemed heresy to Jewish Christians like Peter. But Peter listened and got the message (Acts 10). The Spirit told the two leaders of the church in Antioch, Saul and Barnabas, to leave on a missionary journey. How foolish! Who would then lead the church in Antioch? But the church fasted and prayed, discerned the Spirit's voice, and sent them on their way.

Through the centuries, God has used people to do great things and to do unexpected things. One can list the "great figures" of Church history, and in nearly every case they are still remembered because they "went against the flow." We do not remember and study dull, commonplace bureaucrats who simply maintain the status quo.

So, in our day, we must listen to the Spirit and do what he says, whether it appears foolish or not. And, sadly, those in authority are often the ones who so vociferously defend the hardened, institutionalized system.

I know of a mission church, begun in a thriving suburban area, which could not get support and resources from its local denominational jurisdiction until it bought land for a building. To those denominational executives, "starting a church" included "buying land." They could not see the great potential for growth that was slipping by; they would not consider alternative systems. They were not about to support anything that had any whiff of "foolishness" or "risk."

It is difficult to lead a group of people to accept a challenge—a vision—particularly when the method departs from the accepted pattern. But that is sometimes the Spirit's way. Jesus said that the wind of the Spirit blows where it wishes (John 3:8). If we open the windows of our institutions and structures, the Spirit can blow there. If we do not, it will blow elsewhere.

Granted, churches should not be frivolous with God's money. Granted, there is nothing particularly spiritual about doing dumb things. But the New Testament's warning is not "be cautious." It is "stop quenching the Spirit."

Perhaps, to be honest, we should examine why we resist the Spirit's "foolishness." May it be because we are so unspiritual, so carnal and human, that we cannot sense his leadership?

4. Any movement or progress (that is, change) will provoke opposition.

The story is told of a small Baptist church in Mayfield County, Kentucky, which in the late 1800s had only two deacons. These two irascible fellows hated each other, and if one favored some proposal, the other's opposition was guaranteed. One week the first deacon put a small wooden peg in the back wall of the frame church building so that the preacher-boy could hang his hat there on Sunday. When the second deacon saw the peg the next Sunday, he demanded to know who had done such a thing without consulting him. The church members took sides and the church eventually split. And to this day, the story goes, you can find in Mayfield County, Kentucky, the Anti-peg Baptist Church.

Those of us who have been involved in church life laugh at that story, but we have to laugh to keep from crying. Though the example is so ludicrous as to bring laughter, we know how true it is. No matter what a church leader tries to do, wherever he tries to lead, there will be opposition.

I can remember, when I was younger, thinking (naïvely) that if I loved Jesus and if everyone else in the church loved Jesus, everything would be fine. The ministry would be the most lovely job in the world. That bubble was popped very quickly as I heard church members complain and even fight about the hymns that were sung, the type of preaching the pastor did, the color of the new paint for the fellowship hall, the cost of taking teenagers to new discipleship conferences, and so forth, *ad infinitum*. Christians are people, and people are gripers.

The Lord was angry with the children of Israel in the Exodus because they "murmured"; they griped and complained (Exod. 15-17). They doubted the Lord's leadership. They thought they knew better than God what should be done. In the New Testament, the Lord's brother pronounces judgment on those who are "grumblers and faultfinders" (Jude 16), and Paul warns the Corinthians "not to grumble" (1 Cor. 10:10). He told the Philippians to do whatever they did "without complaining or arguing" (Phil. 2:14), and the Lord's other brother wrote:

> But if you harbor bitter envy and selfish ambition in your hearts, do not boast about it or deny the truth. Such "wisdom" does not come down from heaven but is earthly, unspiritual, of the devil. For where you have envy and selfish ambition, there you find disorder and every evil practice (James 3:14–16).

Some people, I suppose, oppose change just because it *is* change. I have seen Christians in a church business meeting become quite angry because of a suggestion that the old pews be replaced during a sanctuary renovation. They were not particularly spiteful people. They were not against spending money. They just had an emotional attachment to those pews, which they had paid for. They opposed change just because it was change.

Other people oppose change because they resent authority. Whatever "they" (the leaders) want to do is wrong and should be resisted. These people have emotional hang-ups that inhibit their normal functioning. They live with an "us versus them" mentality and a persecution complex ("they're out to get us").

I'm not arguing that Christians should just be docile sheep who do whatever the leaders say. I'm not saying that every idea of the leaders comes from God. I'm saying that these ideas must be tested and prayed over and, if they are from the Lord, be enacted. But don't expect easy sledding. There will be opposition. The only way to avoid it is to do nothing; but then there would be people complaining about *that*!

The point, I believe, is that we must *do* what the Spirit leads us to do. We must not let the belligerents run the church, even if they are important contributors, even if we hate conflict. We must be wise, gentle, and long-suffering. But we must also be obedient and bold to do the Lord's bidding.

People

5. *People matter.*

Perhaps it seems unnecessary to remind ourselves in the Church that people matter, but it often seems to be forgotten.

Church-staff ministers sometimes seem to have their focus obscured as to what matters in church work. Some seem to think that "their" programs are what matter. Some horrendous turf battles have occurred in church-staff meetings when a minister felt that "his" program was being jeopardized.

Other ministers seem to think that what matters are so-called results, (usually defined in terms of how many bodies we can get into the building). When this is the case, any method that works is justified. It sometimes appears that we don't care so much about the *people,* but that they represent a form of success for the ministers.

Other ministers appear to think that what matters is their climbing the ladder, getting a promotion. Whatever is needed to get the people in and get the minister some limelight is used. This may neglect and even hurt people, but that is okay. With this approach, the people are *not* what matters.

But even the most basic reflection about Jesus and the Bible reminds us that God has acted to redeem *people*, that he loves *people*, that each one of us matters to him. The prophets warn Israel of God's judgment because they have not loved people (*see* Amos 4:1–3, 5:11–13), James repeats it (2:1–11, 3:14–16), and Paul tells us that without love for people, we have missed it all (1 Cor. 13:1–3). We may build large churches and impress many people, but if we are selfish or results-oriented rather than people-centered, God will judge us.

6. People are made for relationships and love.

Gary Smalley and John Trent remind us in their book *The Blessing* that each one of us has a deep, innate longing to be loved and accepted. The first setting for this to occur (for most people) is their family. Psychiatrist Scott Peck asserts:

> The feeling of being valuable—"I am a valuable person"—is essential to mental health and is a cornerstone of self-discipline. It is a direct product of parental love. Such a conviction must be gained in childhood; it is extremely difficult to acquire it during adulthood.[2]

He continues that people's sense of self-worth and trust in the safety of one's existence:

> . . . are ideally acquired through the self-discipline and consistent, genuine caring of their parents; they are the most precious gifts of themselves that mothers and fathers can bequeath. When these gifts have not been proffered by one's parents, it is possible to acquire them from other sources, but in that case the process of their acquisition is invariably an uphill struggle, often of lifelong duration and often unsuccessful.[3]

It is now almost a truism that most emotional and psychological problems stem from a low sense of self-worth.

The effects of living in a family that does not give "the blessing"—its love and acceptance—are profound. Without a sense of being valuable, children become adults who are:

the seekers

the shattered

the smotherers

the angry

the detached

the driven,

the seduced.[4]

Your church is full of people like this. The ministers at your church may very likely be like this (many people enter the ministry because they have a great need for approval and acceptance). And, sadly, many of our churches play a large role in continuing to produce people like this. It is one of the world's greatest anomalies that Christian people and Christian churches communicate to their own that they are *not* loved, are *not* good, are *not* people of worth. But we do. Peck remarks that he used to say that the Roman Catholic Church kept him in business as a psychiatrist; he then adds that he could have mentioned any other denomination.

So what is the church's role in all this? Is the church supposed to creep along, holding the hand of all these maladjusted people? What about preaching the gospel? What about living it?

That precisely is the point. The gospel tells us that God loves us, that we are important to him, that we have worth because God has said so. If we *would* preach the gospel, the "Good News" that God loves us in spite of our sins, we would be a source of healing for the troubled multitudes who crowd into our churches.

Then we in the Church must *live* the gospel. We must learn to live in joyous freedom as ones who are ultimately loved and accepted by God, and we must learn to love other people in the same way. It *is* possible to "acquire the blessing" later in life, even if our parents did not give it to us. But it must begin with knowing that God forgives and loves us (with conversion) and it matures with being loved by others. And here the local church can do much.

I don't mean by all this that God's moral expectations should not be preached and taught. I'm not advocating that we all just love each other and revel in our sinfulness. I'm saying that a basic principle of church life should be what the New Testament pounds away at us over and over: "Love one another."

So, hug the kids in your church. Joke and laugh with the teenagers. Take time to talk to older persons. Give the blessing. People are made for relationships and love.

7. *The church must put people into,* *not take them out of, important things.*

I've lately been saying that I have proof that the Almighty is not an evangelical, because the Almighty said that we are to rest on the Sabbath; "committed" evangelicals do anything *but* rest on the Sabbath.

That's a bit of a wisecrack, but just a bit. Most evangelical churches overprogram their people's time. The problem is not that our churches (or should we really say, the ministers?) expect some time commitment from people; it is that we expect our people to spend so much of their time *in unimportant but churchy things.*

According to the Bible, there is to be a rhythm to life. There is to be hard, honest work. There is to be the love and nurture of the family. There is to be worship and service of God. There is to be enjoyment of rest and leisure.

Certainly Christians should worship God each week. We should spend time in fellowship and sharing life with other believers. We should study the Scriptures. But what is amazing is how many Christians are very busy about church work, spending hours at the church building, but feel that they have been working rather than worshiping, fellow-shiping, or learning. We have substituted busyness for reality and depth.

In the West, and in Western evangelical Christianity, we are consumed with activism. We value those who produce. We ask each other, "Are you staying busy?" And we define Christianity in the same terms: busyness, going, doing, helping, serving, sacrificing. The committed core group of the church does most of the work, and finally burnout comes. It comes because the things for which we expect people to sacrifice other important things are themselves not very important; we finally realize it, and we rebel, quit, drop out, "take a rest." Michael Green reports that as David Watson, Anglican pastor in York, lay dying of cancer in 1984, he was still learning the truth that God wants our love more than our service, our hearts rather than our activism.[5]

Are all the meetings in your church necessary? Are the programs doing any good? Are they worth taking people out of family time, out of rest, out of time for their lost neighbors? We preach to our congregations that the family is falling apart and that it is a great tragedy, but we expect that "serious" Christians will be at meetings at church at least three nights a week (Sunday, visitation night, mid-week meeting night). We preach to our congregations to "win the lost," but our people have no time to meet any lost people; they're at church in meetings all the time. Further, the meetings are very structured, so there's little spontaneous loving, sharing, praying, laughing; it's mostly sitting and listening. And if people miss the meetings, we make them feel guilty. Small wonder that many of our people drop out.

In our small, rural congregation, I made a very bold step one summer. I suggested that one Sunday each month be "Family Day." There would be no evening activities, organizations, or worship. People were encouraged, after morning worship, to spend the day with their families. Though everyone was overjoyed at the idea of a Sunday night "off" each month, no one at first wanted to admit that they approved of it. It might be seen as "laziness" or "lack of commitment." Some argued that we would be "encouraging people to miss church." I replied that the people whose weak commitment might be hurt by "an evening off" didn't come in the evening anyway. I didn't mention that I wasn't so insecure about the gospel's or the Holy Spirit's power that I felt that I had to keep everyone under a tight rule and a load of guilt. As people got accustomed to the idea, they began to share their excitement. It was a novel idea, the church allowing people to rest, relax, and be with their families. When the autumn came, the church voted to continue Family Day, and it is still going today.

I'm not campaigning to stop Sunday-evening services. I'm not asking for a lessened commitment. I'm not asking the church to condone minimal Christianity. I'm reminding us that time and family are precious, and that the church has no right to take people away from important things for the sake of trivial things that may seem religious.

8. We must recognize that all of people's deep needs are not "religious."

As an adolescent and young adult, I experienced a lot of guilt; preachers regularly denounced the moods, feelings, and questions I was having as sinful and dangerous. It wasn't for several years that I learned a bit about developmental psychology and saw that the feelings and thoughts I was experiencing were *perfectly normal* for a person my age. As I struggled with deep needs and feelings, my pastors said "be more dedicated" or "read the Bible more." They did not realize that my deep needs were not all religious needs. Paul Tournier asks:

> How does it happen that there are so many depressed individuals among the most fervent believers? And also, how does it happen that so often their faith, which (as my colleague thought) could

be a factor in recovery, appears to further complicate their case, because they reproach themselves for their depression, as if it were a matter of lack of faith?

We see how these relationships between spiritual life and psychological health are subtle and delicate. They must be envisioned in their complexity. We must take account of the importance both of religious life and of the pathological phenomena which science studies.[6]

In the church we seem to sometimes have a problem realizing that people are people, not religious automatons. People have deep, primal fears, needs, and anxieties. Most of these are formed in us in our earliest years, and many of them are unconscious. They are the *result* of sin, in that they are a part of life in a fallen world; they are not sins. For example, a person may not have been loved as a child in a way he could accept. He may be very insecure, frightened of love and relationships. He may be married and thus punishing his wife and children by his aloofness and inability to love. He has profound needs, and Christ can make a tremendous (perhaps the only) difference in his life. This need is deeply spiritual, a matter of the spirit; it is not overtly religious. Just "reading the Bible" won't solve this problem, nor will going to more church meetings.

We must learn that the power of the Holy Spirit can solve any problem or need; we must learn that "being religious" or being "more dedicated" may not. I have experienced what some call "emotional healing," when I literally fell on my face in weakness before God. Going to more church services did not do it. Talking about religion didn't do it. God did it. It was personal, it was "real-life," it was existential. It had little to do with religious structures and programs. It was the raw, naked power of God relating to a raw, naked human soul.

A principle of church life is that we must soft-peddle the religious structures and pat answers. We must spotlight the power of God and the need of the person. People need

God, desperately. They do not necessarily need all of our canned "religious" stuff.

9. People are different.

Of course we all know that people are different. Some are tall, some short. Some are thin, some are not. Some have one color of skin, some another.

But this is not what I mean. I mean that people are *really* different and that this must be taken into account in the church's programming and ministry.

Erik Erikson, for example, has demonstrated that people at different ages are concerned with different issues. In this psychosocial development, infants (birth to age two) are dealing with basic trust versus basic mistrust. They are forming impressions that will likely remain with them forever, about whether the world is a friendly place to be, whether life can be trusted and thus enjoyed. They form deep convictions then about hope. At ages two to three the child deals with autonomy versus shame and doubt. This child is beginning to have some autonomy, some power, some choice, some will. The child has a sense of self, of felt boundaries. This is crushed when the child is shamed, when his autonomy is crushed, and his vulnerability exposed. At ages four to six the child must face the issue of initiative versus guilt. The child now becomes a planner, who begins to sense purpose. At ages seven to twelve the child must deal with industry versus inferiority, or with competence. In ages thirteen to twenty-one the adolescent faces the issue of identity versus role confusion. During the period of ages twenty-one to thirty-five young adults struggle with intimacy versus isolation. From ages thirty-five to sixty adults work with productiveness versus stagnation. After age sixty older adults must face the question of integrity versus despair.[7] The people in your church then are grappling with profound life issues, *and the issues differ according to the ages of the persons.*

Daniel Levinson of Yale Medical School has done a similar study of adults.[8] There are eras in adult life with transitional stages in between. Ages three to seventeen are the Childhood and Adolescence period. Then, after a transition, the person goes into Early Adulthood (ages twenty-two to forty). Following another transition comes Middle Adulthood (ages forty-five to sixty). Another transition leads into Late Adulthood (age sixty-five on). In each era, and in each transition, people must wrestle with different developmental tasks. These seem overwhelming, and often do overwhelm people.

The point for church ministry is this: are you aware that people of different ages face different issues and problems? Do you program so that everyone sees the power and relevance of the gospel *for the problems they are facing?* I'm afraid that many ministers simply preach, teach, or program to answer the needs that *they* are facing, or perhaps the problems of the developmental stage that they have just left. We often assume that everyone is where we are. But they aren't. People of different ages are facing different issues.

But people are different in another way, too. James Fowler has shown that people are at different stages of faith, that is, they view life, religion, and ultimate issues of value and meaning in different ways.[9] There are identifiable stages of these, he argues, that are tied loosely to a chronological development. In adulthood, however, persons might be at any of several levels. Stage One is Intuitive-Projective Faith (early childhood) in which a child can be powerfully influenced by examples, moods, and stories of the faith of important adults. Stage Two (ages six to twelve) is Mythical-Literal Faith, in which the older child separates reality from make-believe. The stories of the faith community become more important. Stage Three (ages twelve and beyond) is Synthetic-Conventional Faith, where the person's developing self-identity leads the person to seek unity of belief with others, and where God is viewed as a close personal friend. This is the stage of the youth group. Most adults

who are in church, Fowler adds, are also here. Stage Four
(early adulthood and beyond) is Individuative-Reflective
Faith, where the self is separated from the group and one
takes greater personal responsibility for one's faith. Analytical, critical thinking begins. Stage Five (midlife and beyond) is Conjunctive Faith, where deeper self-awareness
comes and the person is open to paradox and the depth of
reality. Stage Six (midlife and beyond) is Universalizing
Faith, reached by very few people. Here issues of love and
justice become central, as does the radical living out of the
kingdom of God. These are the Mother Teresas, the Ghan-
dis, the Martin Luther King, Jrs.

The point is that, it seems to me, most evangelical church
programming is aimed at the Stage Three level. This is the
"average" church member. The depth of analysis and understanding is, honestly, quite superficial. "Youth group piety"
is seen as the norm. We're trying to get our church people
to do what we're trying to get the teenagers (newly into
Stage Three) to do: realize that God is to be part of our
lives each day, not just Sunday; read the Bible; pray; be
consistently moral. Evangelical churches are good at re-
cruiting people into faith and leading them to "youth group
piety" (Stage Three); we're not good at leading them beyond it, and we don't know what to do with people who
are beyond it. Indeed, people past Stage Three are usually
considered troublemakers and malcontents who have an
attitude problem. This comes because they, thinking ana-
lytically, see the problems and superficiality of the average
church, and they express their frustration with it. To a minister who is himself at Stage Three, these people are quite
threatening.

But we must realize that people at different stages of
faith must all be ministered to. The church's programming
must be planned with breadth in mind; we must try to
provide help and growth for people *wherever they are* on
the faith journey, rather than trying to force everyone into
one mold. This is more difficult and requires more effort,

but it must be done. Otherwise we lose people who are not "average."

But it goes on. People are different in still other ways. The Southern Baptist Sunday School Board's research shows that the USA population (and Southern Baptist church membership) can be divided into nine groups: Belongers, Achievers, Survivors, Sustainers, Emulators, I-Am-Me persons, Experientials, Societally Conscious, and Integrated. The study showed that 82 percent of Southern Baptists are Belongers and Achievers, compared to only 58 percent of the general population. In other words, Southern Baptist churches attract Belongers and Achievers. James Williams, executive vice-president of the Baptist Sunday School Board notes that "We tend to perpetuate outreach methods that work with Belongers and Achievers."[10] Most programs and worship styles are aimed at these two groups, for they are the constituency who are there and whom the ministers must keep happy.

The United Methodist Church's General Board of Discipleship conducted its own survey that identified five types of audiences in their congregations: Fellowship, Traditional, Study, Social Concerns, and Multiple Interest Group.[11]

What do we conclude from these studies? United Methodist executive Hartman asserts "It is essential that we recognize that a very real and deeply based diversity does exist among lay persons in most local congregations."[12] Southern Baptist executive Williams notes:

> While Southern Baptists have in common such things as conservative theology and a strong belief in biblical authority, there are also many differences. It is not possible to draw a composite picture of a typical Southern Baptist. Through sharing and involvement we must identify real needs rather than deal with perceived needs.[13]

In our church ministry, we must stop trying to stamp people with our cookie-cutter molds. People are different, with different outlooks, interests, and viewpoints.

I'm not suggesting that each person can shape the gospel any way he wants it. The gospel does not change. Christianity does not change. But people are not all like you. Their views and feelings must be respected and valued, and they must be ministered to.

10. We must take the gifts of the Spirit seriously.

In the last twenty years, thanks to the charismatic renewal, evangelicals have become aware of the gifts of the Spirit. We have had seminars, sermon series, and retreats on the subject until we don't want to hear any more about it. Just because we have finally learned about spiritual gifts, however, doesn't necessarily mean that we structure church life and ministry around them. But we must.

There is much literature available on the gifts of the Holy Spirit.[14] Without belaboring the issue here, let us just say that, in the New Testament, Paul teaches that Christians have "spiritual gifts."

The major passages are 1 Corinthians 12 and 14, Romans 12:4–8, and Ephesians 4:11–13. (This last passage deals more with roles or ministries given to the church than with gifts given to individual Christians). In the main passage, 1 Corinthians 12, Paul makes several points:

1. It is the same Holy Spirit who gives the different gifts (vv. 4–6).
2. It is the Holy Spirit who gives the gifts (vv. 7, 11).
3. The Holy Spirit gives the gifts "for the common good" of the church (v. 7).
4. Each person in the church, and the gifts he has, are necessary (vv. 14–26).

In the same passage, there are two clusters of gifts/roles, one in verses 8–10, the other in verses 28–30. The gifts mentioned are:

1. word (or message) of wisdom
2. word (or message) of knowledge
3. faith
4. healing
5. miraculous powers
6. prophecy
7. ability to distinguish between spirits
8. ability to speak in different kinds of tongues
9. interpretation of tongues
10. teaching
11. helping
12. administration

Romans 12 adds three other gifts: encouraging, contributing to the needs of others, and showing mercy. Ephesians 4:11 adds one further gift/role, that of evangelist.

While there are differences of opinion about what all these gifts are and whether some are still operative today, it seems that in the Church we must take seriously that the Spirit gives gifts and that they are to be used for the common good of the Church. And church ministry should be focused around them.

For example, preachers continually harangue church members to win the lost, and all church members *should* be witnesses. But some have the spiritual gift from God of evangelism, of sharing the gospel and winning the lost. People with this gift should be set aside for this task. They should be taken off the Centennial Anniversary Committee and allowed (and encouraged) to do what they are gifted to do. Others have the gift of teaching, which I believe means the ability to spiritually help or nurture other Christians. It does not mean the ability to give a lecture. People with this gift should be freed from other responsibilities (for which they may not be gifted), so that they can function in their area of giftedness. How are the new Christians in our midst to be nurtured if we keep the nurturers tied up with Building and Grounds Committee meetings?

But there are members in your church who have gifts of administration (organizing) and helping. Let them maintain the building and grounds. Stop making them feel guilty because they are not comfortable with direct evangelistic visitation or with teaching a Sunday-school class.

And, finally, we must let the Spirit organize our ministries around the gifts he gives. That is, in the Church there are evangelizers, nurturers, leaders, helpers, and so forth. This should provide the structure for our local church and ministry. Often, though, we approach all this like a business or the government. We are task-oriented, not gift-oriented. We look around and say, "The building's falling apart. Let's get some people to work on this." People are then nominated to form another committee. Or, we say, "We have six vacancies in our Sunday-school faculty. Let's fill those slots!" The structure we have, the organization that is already rolling, determines the needs and requirements.

Should we not say, "Who are our nurturers, those who have the gift of spiritual teaching? Let's put them into situations (Sunday-school classes or not) where they can nurture?" Or, instead of saying, "We've got to get more people out for visitation," to say "Who are our evangelizers? Let's find them, encourage them, provide them opportunities to exercise their gifts?" Or, "Who has the gift of leadership? Let them guide us," rather than saying "Let's find someone for a straitjacket slot we have determined to fill."

It may seem a small difference, because even if we begin with the gifts we must still get organized. But it is an important difference. It allows the Spirit to raise up (and suppress) ministries. It's the difference between three women in a Sunday-school class saying "We have the gifts of mercy and helping. We would like to use them by opening a clothes closet" and the church "board" saying, "First Church has a clothes closet. Shouldn't we have one? Let's start one."

For the Spirit's life to flow through us, we must take seriously the gifts of the Spirit.

Programming

11. The Church's primary task is not its own organizational growth.

Many pastors and church members today would say that the Church's primary task is to grow. In my own denomination, nearly every convention sermon or resolution has to do with growth. Church-staff meetings often deal with "How can we grow more?" or "If we do this, how will it affect our growth?" Church-growth consultants and super-church pastors tell the rest of us that, if we want our churches to grow, we must always keep before the people the emphasis on growth.

But the Church's (and your church's) primary task is not to extend your organizational structure, to have more classes and programs, more people and money. That is *not* our essential task. Our essential task is to be obedient to Christ.

Joseph Ton is a Romanian Baptist preacher. Recently, at a conference in Texas, he told of leaving Romania and illegally remaining abroad. He journeyed to Oxford for a time of study and was then preparing to return to Romania. As he described for a Christian student group in Oxford his plans, a student said, "Joseph, that is all very nice. But, realistically, what chance of success do you think you have?" Ton noted that he considered that to be a typically Western question: "What chance of success?" He added that he did not think in terms of success; he thought in terms of *obedience*.

Joseph Ton is right. In the West, we think in capitalist economic terms. We think in terms of success. We like winners, we want to be winners. And in ministerial circles, to be a winner is to have the biggest church. So we set out to get one.

I am not negating the importance of evangelism. I believe that if we are obedient to the Lord, we will be witnessing and people will be saved. I'm not making excuses for churches that go for months and years without a profession of faith. I believe that people are really lost, that Jesus really saves, and that we must share the Good News. What I am saying is that the ministers are probably much more concerned about "how many we had in Sunday school" than the Lord is. We have become Organization Men, the Organization has become our lives, our success or failure is measured by it, and it is what matters most to us. When we see our ministerial friends at a meeting and they ask "How are things going?", we immediately tell them about The Organization: "Two hundred in Sunday school, youth group growing, new staff member," et cetera, et cetera. When crucial issues come before us, we often selfishly consider how our possible responses "will affect attendance," for instance. It is depressing to see how often ministerial esteem shapes church policy and goals.

I know of a youth minister who refused to confront a teenager in his youth group about her publicly-known promiscuity because her parents were prominent citizens and church members. He did not make his decision based on his concern for her, that he was afraid confrontation might drive her away. He made the decision based on self-interest, based on what effect it would have on him, his job, his advancement, the Organization.

I know of a high school that is far too small for its growing city, but the school board has vetoed a second high school; it would dilute the talent for the football team. Similarly, I know of churches that could start needed mission churches, but they won't. It would mean the loss of good workers and a drop in attendance and offering receipts. The Organization is more important than extending the kingdom.

The Church should grow. Lost people need to be saved. Inactive Christians need encouragement to "reenlist." But it is a different matter to plan church activities and programs around ways to expand the organization, to use any method that "works." Being obedient to Christ is what matters, and that may at times hurt your organization's upward trajectory. Jesus declared that we are his friends if we *keep his commandments,* not if we start a new Sunday-school class. Growth is *not* all that the Lord cares about.

12. *Programs exist for people, not vice versa.*

One of the many errors made by President Richard Nixon in the Watergate era was that he forgot the role of government. He apparently concluded that government did not exist for the people's welfare, but that it existed for its own welfare, regardless of the people's need.

Jesus had the same problem with the Pharisees. One Sabbath Jesus' disciples picked some heads of grain as they walked through a field. The Pharisees pounced, telling Jesus that they had violated the Sabbath law forbidding work on the Sabbath. Jesus cited an Old Testament example of the same thing and added, "The Sabbath was made for man, not man for the Sabbath" (Mark 2:23–28).

Jesus was saying that God gave the Sabbath to be a day of rest and worship for his people. The people's need (cessation from labor) was the cause for the creation of Sabbath. The Pharisees reversed this. They said that what mattered was the holy day; people existed to keep the laws pertaining to it. The important thing to them was the Sabbath and its laws of observance. God's original concern for people's need was forgotten.

We sometimes do this in church life. We forget that what matters to God is the people and that their needs be met. We assume that what matters is the church, the structures, and the programs. People are important only insofar as they are needed to staff and attend the programs.

Once a program has been started, it takes on a life of its own. It must be maintained and staffed and attended. What begins as a response to a need (for instance, children's choirs) becomes an end in itself. At one time someone saw that the children in the church needed to be trained to sing—but now it's just another program that we have to attend.

I have a good friend with young children. He is a seminary student who works twenty hours each week and spends a lot of time studying. His wife is a public-school teacher who is working on her master's degree at night. As you gather, they don't have a lot of free family time. In fact, with their schedules, Wednesday night was the only weeknight that the whole family could be together. So the parents decided not to send their children to children's choir at church on Wednesday night. They would have a nice dinner at home and then do something together as a family. It wasn't long before the children's choir worker stopped the mom one Sunday and "read her the riot act" for not sending the children to choir. She did not ask if things were all right, she did not wonder if the children needed the evening with the family more than with her. Children's choir had taken on a life of its own. It existed and it was to be attended and the mom was supposed to send her kids so that the church could have a big children's choir. It didn't matter that children's choir was not a need in the children's lives. Their need was secondary; the program had become primary. "Man is made for the Sabbath," she meant.

Some people need encouragement to attend programs. Sometimes a nudge or a suggestion is proper. But we must get the focus, as Jesus did, off the programs and back on the people. We must stop deciding what people need and then telling them to come and making them feel guilty if they don't come. We must begin to listen to the Holy Spirit and the people and discover the needs, and then we must structure programs that meet those needs. We must stop making people into cogs in a machine.

Therefore we must not expect every person to attend every program. Perhaps we should offer lots of programs, lots of places for different needs to be met. But we must stop assuming that every person needs to be at every program. They don't. Maybe *you* do; that doesn't mean that *they* do. People pick programs and ministries according to their needs and gifts. Some Christians who attend Bible study on Sunday morning, hear two biblical (dare we hope?) sermons on Sunday, and attend midweek Bible study, do *not* need to go to another Bible study on Thursday. Some Christian women may get along just fine and be right with God *without* needing to go to the Women's Missionary Club. Besides that—it leads to burnout.

I recall reading a few years ago an interview with the pastor of a large downtown church in a metro area. He said that the staff had had to work very hard and become very creative to get people to come back downtown for Sunday-night activities, but that it still wasn't working. Do you see his thinking? There *were* Sunday night activities and people were *supposed* to come, so ways had to be found to *get* them to come. The main concern seemed to be for the programs.

We must stop being slaves to our programs. *They are to be our servants, not the other way around.* Programs exist for people.

13. We must not equate "being a disciple" with "going to meetings."

I can clearly remember hearing a man in our Baptist church say one night in a discussion group, "I don't know what more the Lord expects of me. I'm at church two nights a week as it is." He wasn't kidding. He meant it. Though he was a good man—at least on the surface—his conception of being a Christian and serving God was "coming to meetings at the church." That's what it meant to be a disciple of Jesus.

We have nurtured this in our evangelical churches. In recent years I have noticed how—usually—in sermons that plead for more dedication and commitment, the application comes around to attendance at church meetings: "If you'll get right with God, you'll start coming to the Wednesday-night-prayer meeting." In our churches we categorize people by their commitment (that is, attendance) level. The superficial Christians come only Sunday morning (I've even heard them called "holy once'ers"—those who come once a week); the more committed also come to Sunday-evening service, and the serious people even come Wednesday night for prayer meeting. And we church leaders let this idea go on, for it helps (we think) the attendance.

Certainly, people who want to follow Christ need to worship and fellowship with other Christians. We all know that Lone Ranger Christians do not survive. But we have pitched "Christian commitment" at the lowest possible level: *showing up for meetings.* If you come, you're committed; if you don't, you're not.

We must begin to think and teach about what it means to follow Jesus at a deeper level than this. What does being a Christian have to do with the way you treat your spouse, love your children, do your job, view political factors, conduct business affairs? Being committed enough to attend meetings is the bare nursery floor of discipleship. "Going to meetings" is not the same as walking in the Spirit, loving your neighbor as yourself, obeying God's commandments, or honoring Christ in all we do.

14. We must not proliferate programs just because we can.

In his account of attempted church renewal at Our Heritage Wesleyan Church in Scottsdale, Arizona, Bob Girard tells of thinking that a successful church program meant one where the lights were burning at the church every night of the week.[15] The health and vitality of the church was to be measured by the number of programs. With this mentality, it follows, one can never do enough. There are always more programs that some other church somewhere is doing.

But some of our churches are like Girard's. We equate activism with "success."

And when we hire additional staff members, it gets worse. Staff members like to have programs to administer. I suppose we in the churches have fostered this, for this is how we measure a minister's effectiveness: how many programs he is running. If there are a lot of people at church a lot of the time for activities and meetings we assume that the church is healthy, spiritual, and growing. It is much more difficult, of course, to evaluate what is *actually* going on in people's lives, how the Lord is at work with us, whether what we are doing at church is helping people. So, when in doubt, start a new program!

I know that people are helped by participating in programs. I'm not advocating the elimination of all church activities. I'm asking that we have a good reason for starting a program and spending the money and people's time. I'm asking that we not proliferate programs just because we can. I'm asking us to remember again that people's needs should determine the programs we have.

15. If a program cannot sustain itself without "propping up" by the staff, we should let it die.

Girard tells us that this rule was employed in their congregation. The result?

> Three choirs died within two months! Along with mid-week service and several committees. Within eighteen months, the Women's Missionary Society was gone—we were down to one business meeting of any kind each month and another choir was about to bite the dust.[16]

These are frightening figures to a "success-minded" minister or church leader. But it represents the truth, doesn't it? How many of our programs and activities just struggle along? How many would whimper and die if the ministerial staff stopped propping them up with pressure to attend?

How many meetings do you attend that you do not enjoy, seem to meet no need, and you wish you could avoid?

Some people will not let us intimidate them. If they do not want to attend a meeting, they just don't come. But others of us are too afraid of offending the pastor or our church friends, or we operate with a huge load of guilt and are thus afraid of God—so we keep coming to meaningless meetings. Someone decided long ago that such a program should exist. People came. It met a need. Then times changed; the program became superfluous. But as we noted earlier, programs take on a life of their own. It's almost like the title of a horror film: *The Program That Wouldn't Die.* We go on and on with it, supporting it, propping it up.

I believe that the Holy Spirit will show us what to do in our church life. I believe that he will tell us which programs to start and which ones to stop. I believe that programs exist for people's needs, and that if you want to know if a program is meeting needs, you count heads. People vote with their feet.

We must not keep on having a program just to be having it. We must be open to the Spirit's leading. We must be open to a redirecting of institutional energy. We must stop trying to decide for everyone (including the Spirit) what people need.

If a program is so meaningless that people won't come without hype and pressure from the staff, let it go.

16. *We must distinguish between fundamental, essential tasks and historically conditioned methods.*

Ralph Neighbour, Jr., remarks, slightly tongue-in-cheek, that the Seven Last Words of the Church are "We never tried it that way before."[17] He makes a powerful point. We in the churches get locked into certain methods and ways of doing things. We canonize the methods. We think that the *way* we have chosen to do a task is as important and unchanging as the *task* itself.

We must avoid this mistake. There are unchanging, central tasks for the Church to perform: worship, evangelism, nurture, love for the brethren, service. These *must* be done. The nature of the Church requires the performance of these works. But *how we go about doing them* is quite another matter.

Most of us do not have enough historical perspective to see that *all* our church methods are historically conditioned, that is, they arose in a particular time in a particular culture to meet a particular need. They were appropriate for their time and place. However, they may not now be the best way of accomplishing the task.

For example, on the American frontier, church was as much a social phenomenon as a religious one. People lived harsh lives, marked by hard work and isolation from other families. When the day for church rolled around (maybe every other Sunday, when the preacher came), it was a big event. Families traveled by wagon or walked to the meeting place. After "preaching" was over, the ladies spread out the food that they had brought. After lunch, the adults, who hadn't seen any other adults for days, talked. Maybe there was "singing." People who had made such an effort to come to church, and who so enjoyed seeing other people, stayed all day. In the evening there was "preaching" again, then everyone went home.

We no longer live on the frontier, with that kind of social milieu or interaction, but we still make church an all-day Sunday affair. In the church where I worship, there is a prayer meeting at 8:30, Sunday school at 9:30, and morning worship at 10:45. That takes all morning. Most Sundays some group has a luncheon at the church. The earliest activities in the afternoon begin at 4:00 and the worship service is over at 7:30-8:00. That amounts to almost all day.

The point, now, is why do we "do" church this way? Does the New Testament command us to meet for several hours on Sunday? No. Does the New Testament order us to worship again on Sunday night? No. Then why do we do it? Because our frontier heritage said that this was an effective way to do it. For Christians on the frontier, living far apart, isolated from contact with others, bound by hard work, Sunday was the only time of the week to leave the farm, go somewhere, worship, be taught, and have fellowship. They found a way to do the important things. But is this the best way to do things now? Can we see—and will we admit—that the methods are not sacred or permanent? Can we admit that Bible study is important, but having everyone in the same building at the same time (9:30 Sunday morning) is not? Can we admit that evangelism is crucial, but alternate methods are acceptable? Dare we admit that programs that once were appropriate may not be now, and that new ones are needed?

Several years ago, I was the Sunday-school teacher for the college group at our church. We struggled and struggled. On a good Sunday we had four students come. The lessons were from our denominational materials and were good, but the meetings were boring. Everyone sat around and looked bored like they always had in Sunday school. Eventually some one else took over—with the same result. There followed another teacher—with the same result. Then a couple of college students asked me to lead them in a Bible study during the Wednesday-night-prayer-meeting hour. They didn't feel comfortable going in with the youth group, and they didn't really enjoy the adult meeting. So, I agreed. During the next two years we averaged from fifteen to twenty-five college students at Bible study on Wednesday night! I never made a visit. I never pressured anyone to come. But as we sat in a circle (one that grew larger and larger), talked about our lives, studied the Scriptures, prayed together, and grew to love one another, the Holy Spirit did his work. Lives were touched and changed. New people came. During those months, there were still only two or three at college Sunday school. Why? Sunday morning at 9:30 is the worst time of the week for college students to talk about the Bible. But on a week night, sitting informally in a room that was "theirs," Bible study worked great. By accident we discovered that the old method (Sunday morning, 9:30, sitting in rows with suits and dresses on) wasn't very successful, but that an alternate plan worked very well. But when I left that church to become pastor of another church, the Wednesday-night-college-Bible study was discontinued. Today, there are still three or four at college Sunday school.

Why are we so rigid? Why can we not loosen up? Why can't we hear the Spirit lead us to discard time-worn methods and adopt new ones *that work for us now just as the old ones did for others in another day?* "Don't rock the boat," we're told. "You've got an attitude problem," I hear. But I keep thinking about those three or four in college Sunday school.

All of our church-work methods are historical products. We don't do anything in church life "like the New Testament." Our worship styles are historically developed, our musical tastes, our church architecture, our having church buildings, our programming everything, our having denominations, our educational models, our classes, our youth groups, our retreats and camps—everything! Whatever aspect of church life you pick, there was a time when it was not done the way it is now.

A few months ago, I introduced into our worship services the singing of some praise choruses. One older lady in the church, who was a good friend and strong supporter of mine, told me that she didn't like singing all those new songs that she didn't know. I told her that all the old songs that she loved were at one time new songs that she didn't know. With an awestruck look, she said, "I guess you're right." Now she loves the praise choruses.

Can we stretch and grow? Can we learn that old methods are not sacred? Can we love Christ and the Church so much that we will endure a little discomfort for the sake of more efficient methods? We must, or the Church will become more and more an anachronism, an enclave of (in my case) nineteenth-century Southern culture and piety. All this while the world passes us by, with our three or four in college Sunday school.

We *must* distinguish between fundamental, essential tasks and historically conditioned methods.

17. We must ruthlessly evaluate programs and methods.

Richard Wilke is the United Methodist bishop of the Arkansas area. In a provocative book *And Are We Yet Alive?*, he charts the decline of the United Methodist Church. One of the reasons for the decline, he asserts, is that no one is "minding the store." He cites the remarks of a Christian friend who is chief executive officer of a major corporation:

> "Any large company that has a track record like The United Methodist Church, whose charts show steady decline, would have been called on the carpet long ago. The board of directors would have demanded emergency meetings, and the corporate executives would have been held accountable. Consultants would have been brought in. Heads would roll. It would not be business as usual."[18]

Whether or not we agree that such corporate procedures should be employed in church matters, the point remains: we must evaluate honestly, brutally, the effectiveness of our work. We must tell the truth. We must "tell it like it is." We must call a spade a spade. If programs are not working, let's say so. If the wrong people are in leadership, let's say so. If changes need to be made, let's say so.

In the small church where I served as pastor, the early autumn meant that it was time for the nominating committee to prepare a list of church officials and workers for congregational approval. On the nominating committee was a middle-aged man who had become active in our church in the last year. Problem number one, he probably did not have enough maturity to be on the committee charged with selecting church workers. Problem number two, someone on the committee nominated him as director of our Sunday-school program. Problem number three, I (and some others who knew he did not have the needed maturity) did not want to risk a confrontation or hurt feelings, so we did not contest the suggestion. He took the job (for which he was not prepared), did a poor job, and after several childish, intemperate conflicts with church leaders, took his family out of the church. All this could have been avoided if I (or we) had voiced our opinion. We did not mind the store.

"Whatever happens" in church life is *not* okay. If our methods for doing the Lord's work are inefficient, we must admit it and change them. If personnel changes are needed, let's make them. I take this seriously: when it became apparent to me and other church leaders that I could not (with my seminary responsibilities) do the kind of work needed from the pastor, I resigned.

I'm not advocating a "witch hunt" mentality. I'm not advocating chastising every church worker who is not perfect. I'm saying that the Lord's work is important, and "business as usual" won't do.

If we are going to evaluate the church programs, someone must be the evaluator. This responsibility may be shared with several others, but someone—some group—somewhere—must bite the bullet and tell it like it is. God has appointed leaders in the church whose task is to watch over the spiritual lives of the flock, and those leaders will give an account to God for their work (Heb. 13:17; 1 Peter 5:1–4).

We can't just "rock along." We must ruthlessly evaluate our programs and methods.

Structure and Function

18. We must not assume that God's will is determined by a 51 percent vote.

When Martin Luther appeared before the Diet of Worms (the assembled princes of Germany) in 1521, his opponent taunted him with the question, "Are you the only one who is right?" Luther had attacked the centuries-old traditions and teachings of the Roman Catholic Church, and now the Church was asking him if he alone were right and all the rest of Europe wrong. Brazen as he was, Luther replied that *yes,* he *was* the only one who was right.

It is always lonely going when you buck the tide and disagree with the majority. But in the Lord's work we must not become slaves to the wishes and whims of the crowd.

In free churches like my own, congregational government is upheld as a (if not *the*) cardinal distinctive of proper church life. The theory is that the Holy Spirit will speak to everyone and thus the majority's wish will be the wish of the Spirit.

But it is not that simple. All of us who have lived in congregational-form churches know of situations where votes were manipulated, and what happens when the majority are filled with party spirit and competitiveness? Or sin? I'm afraid the theory of the Spirit leading us all into the same opinion is usually just that: theory. For this, there is a very potent reason: if we are going to be genuinely obedient to Christ, we must disregard our own personal comfort, privilege, and ambition and, humanly speaking, *that will rarely be done by a majority vote.* The majority of a church will not vote to inconvenience themselves. People are sinful and rebellious. If that sounds negative and cynical, chalk it up to my having been involved in church all my life. Bishop Wilke of the United Methodist Church cites democratic control of the churches as one of the evidences of his denomination's problems.[19] The majority favor the status quo, the majority are not analytical, and the majority (in my experience) are not deeply spiritual people of God. A few people in church are; the majority are not. That's just the way it is.

Furthermore (in my opinion) one will scan the pages of the New Testament in vain for wide evidence of majority control of church matters. There is no account of a congregation deciding by majority vote what the will of God was or what "truth" was. There are, on the other hand, numerous references to the apostles' meeting to decide doctrine, apostles giving orders, and apostles overseeing congregations and the Church at large.

The American free-church approach has deeper roots in the out-group's rejection of the establishment's power (for example, Anabaptists and Baptists), a making sacred of the rights of the individual,[20] and the avowal of American democracy than it has in the New Testament. Post-Enlightenment Europe called for the end of the rule of the elite, political or religious. This spirit was cultivated on the American frontier.

This approach finally ends with statements like "We called [hired] the preacher, we can fire him"; or "Since we pay the bills, we'll call the shots." In American political life, this is the model. The people (through their elected representatives) rule. But it is a large assumption to presume that this is how the New Testament church was organized.

I believe that the people of God can be led by the Spirit; I believe that they sometimes are. But I believe that the majority can be, and often is, wrong and out of step with the Spirit's wishes. We must take seriously the gifts of the Spirit, that some have the gift of leadership. We must take seriously the New Testament model that the apostles, gifted by God to lead, *led*. God does not change his views in response to a majority vote, and neither should we.

So then, how do we operate, particularly those of us in the free-church tradition? We must operate the way we actually do. In nearly every church, there is a small group that has the spiritual respect of the congregation. The church body recognizes their spiritual maturity and gifts for leadership. These people lead the church. In congregational polity, the full body finally votes on matters, but it usually approves the recommendations of its leaders. Though most free-church people would faint at the name, it is a practical, functional eldership.

What we must do is to make sure that those whom the church follows are people of the Spirit, of prayer, of spiritual gifts for leadership. These must be the qualifications, *not* that they give a lot of money, or that their family has been in the church for generations, or that they are successful in the business world.

God will make his will known to us, but not always by a 51 percent vote.

19. *There is to be pastoral supervision.*

Most of us in American evangelical churches will not accept a pastoral overseer. We want to do our Christian lives "our way," without interference from anyone, anywhere. Some of us have even been offended when someone at church had the audacity to suggest to us that a part of our lives was not right. "Who does that guy think he is," we fume, "telling *me* how to live?"

We seem to think that the priesthood of the believer means that all Christians are equal in all ways, that whatever we think is right, and that however we live is okay. No one has the authority to tell me—a free person in Christ—about *anything.* So, our churches are full of autonomous, independent, free-wheeling people who receive no guidance. And we ministers fall into the trap, too—we wouldn't dream of making suggestions to a church member about how to live, pointing out potential problems, or actually confronting someone in their sin. It's an "every man for himself" Christianity, with the ministers offering little personal guidance and counseling, and the people not accustomed (or willing) to receive it.

Granted, Jesus did warn about the hypocrisy of pointing out everyone else's problems while being blissfully unaware of one's own (Matt. 7:3–5). Granted, some people are out of line in going around trying to "straighten everyone out." Granted, such overseeing has often been done poorly— but that is not the point. The point is that in the New Testament, Christians were not Lone Rangers who believed and acted any way they wished. Rather, in the Church, God appointed pastors (elders) whose task was the pastoral supervision of the flock. But in our day, ministers and lay people alike quail at the thought of ministerial authority and guidance. That is because our mind-set is shaped by modern Western individualism rather than the New Testament.

The apostles clearly "ran" the Church, under the Spirit's guidance. In the Book of Acts, the apostles (not the whole Church) elected a replacement for Judas (1:20–26). When Philip took the gospel to Samaria, the apostles in Jerusalem sent Peter and John to investigate and preach (8:14–16). When Gentiles in Antioch were converted through the preaching of visitors from Cyprus and Cyrene, the apostles in Jerusalem sent Barnabas to see what was going on. When some Christian teachers began to argue that a person had to be a good Jew (be circumcised, keep the law of Moses) before he could be a Christian, the church in Antioch sent Paul, Barnabas, and some other believers to Jerusalem "to see the apostles and elders about this question" (15:2). When they had arrived, "The apostles and elders met to consider this question" (15:6). When they reached a decision, "the apostles and elders" sent a letter containing their decision to "the Gentile believers in Antioch, Syria, and Cilicia" (15:23). There was pastoral supervision. Believers were not left to make up their own minds and form their own opinions, which they then defended by "the priesthood of the believer."

Paul founded churches and gave them precise instructions in doctrine and morals; he did not ask them what they thought. He told Titus, who was in Crete, to "straighten out what was left unfinished" and to "appoint elders [pastors]" (Titus 1:5). He did not tell Titus to oversee congregational election of pastors, but to *appoint* them. Peter (1 Peter 5:1–4) says that the elders [pastors] are shepherds of the flock, who are under Jesus, the "chief Shepherd." And the writer of Hebrews (13:17) orders the believers:

Obey your leaders and submit to their authority. They keep watch over you as men who must give an account. Obey them so that their work will be a joy, not a burden, for that would be of no advantage to you.

The New Testament is clear, then, that there is to be pastoral oversight. This is not arrogant domination of a congregation by a megalomanic personality, but the loving, gentle but firm, caring guidance of the flock.

This requires spiritual leaders whose gifts of leadership are recognized and accepted by the congregation. It also requires that Christians are put into some structure where they can be known, loved, and cared for. It brings us back to nurturing. It brings us back to small groups of Christians who watch over one another in love, who encourage and help one another. It brings us to the pastors of the church nurturing the group leaders, who nurture those in the groups. If someone flakes out on the church, someone knows and cares. If someone is having problems, someone knows. If someone needs encouragement, someone knows about it. This cannot happen outside of small groups.

I'm not advocating an "iron hand" leadership style; the Scripture speaks strongly against that (1 Peter 5:1–4). I'm not trying to legitimize insecure pastors who have to be "in control." In fact, in the New Testament, spiritual leadership is *shared,* not held by one man.

John Wesley in the eighteenth century had four requirements for persons seeking to be pastoral leaders:

1. Do they know God?
2. Have they received gifts?
3. Have they the graces?
4. Have they produced fruit? Are any truly convinced of sin and converted to God by their preaching?[21]

Meanwhile, Michael Green has succinctly summarized New Testament teaching regarding ministry in the church:

1. Ministry had to be received before it was exercised.
2. All Christians were called to ministry.
3. Ministry was a function not a status.
4. Ministry was corporate and shared.
5. Authorization followed ministry rather than preceded it.
6. Character, not intellect, was the most important condition.
7. Leaders were selected from experienced men.
8. Leaders were trained on the job as apprentices, not in a college.
9. Leaders were of two kinds, local and circulating.
10. Leaders were called to lead and serve in their own locality.
11. Leaders were normally not paid.
12. Leaders practiced an enabling ministry.
13. Doctrine was important.
14. Ministry was seen in terms of people, not buildings.[22]

Though our modern society deplores oversight in any area of life, we must admit that in the early Church there was pastoral supervision.

20. The task of the pastoral team is equipping.

I, like many of you, have seen lots of preachers and churches. The most effective ones have been those pastors who did not try to do all the work themselves. They understood that the work was to be shared by others and that their task as pastors was to oversee and equip the believers.

In the New Testament pastoral leadership is shared. The apostles were a group, and when references are made to elders (pastors) the form is plural. In a congregation there were several people who shared the pastoral leadership and oversight. They pooled their gifts and insights and they acted as a check on the possible errors of another. There is to be, in Christ's Church, shared leadership in a pastoral team.

In the church where I served as pastor, there was such a team. It had begun as a monthly meeting of the former pastor, the Sunday-school director, and the assistant Sunday-school director. The latter two were laymen. This Sunday-school Council met to discuss concerns of the Sunday school: were new classes needed, how were new members being assimilated, how were the teachers doing, did anyone need encouragement or a "breather"? When I became the pastor, this group continued to meet. As the months went by, we found ourselves discussing a broader range of pastoral issues. These men (to whom a third was soon added) *were* the spiritual leaders of the church. No one doubted it. They were looked up to, respected, and often called on for spiritual help. They had, in other words, spiritual gifts for leadership, and the congregation recognized it, though informally. I relied on these men for guidance, insight, and help. I was the only one being paid; I preached the sermons on Sunday; I was "the pastor." But *we* were the pastoral team. I knew it, and they knew it. These men, with no formal training, had tremendous spiritual gifts for ministry. It was the closest thing that I have experienced to the New Testament's idea of a shared, team ministry. And it worked well, both for the church and for me as pastor.

This pastoral team, further, is *not* to do all the work of the church. This is a widely held idea. "We pay the preacher," people say, "to do the church work." But the biblical model is found in Ephesians 4:11–13. God gives spiritual roles to some (apostles, evangelists, prophets, pastors, teachers) whose task is to "equip the saints for the work of ministry." Pastors are *not* to do all the work; they are to help God's people discover and nurture their gifts and find their place of service. Elton Trueblood notes that:

> The older idea was that the lay members were the pastor's helpers, but the new and vital idea is that the pastor is the helper of the

ordinary lay members in the performance of their daily ministry in the midst of secular life.[23]

This is what the pastoral team in a church must focus on. It is not just trying to "get people involved." It is not getting big crowds to come hear the professionals hold forth on theological subjects. It is creating the structures and environment where people's gifts are elicited and nurtured, and where places of ministry (not necessarily empty slots in the organization) are found. We come back again to nurture, and we come back again to small groups led by spiritually gifted and sensitive people.

Bishop Wilke of the United Methodist Church recalled his days as a pastor:

I realized a few years ago that our church was caught up in busy work. At the same time, our active people, especially those under forty, could not understand simple biblical allusions in the sermons. New people were expressing an interest in Bible study. So, we sent several members to study the Bethel Bible Plan [a two-year, Lutheran-conceived course in Bible and theology], and we took the leadership training program. I'll never forget returning to the church with the instruction from Bethel: Set aside the best evening of the week for study. In our church, the best evening was Wednesday when all of our commissions, committees, boards, and councils met. I remember sitting with my associate pastor and a key layperson, looking into one another's eyes and talking. Finally, one of us said, "It's time to put first things first. Housekeeping is second to spiritual formation. Bethel Bible goes on Wednesday; the committees have to meet on Monday." That act alone began a transforming action in the congregation, for soon, after training our leaders for two years, each Wednesday night three to four hundred people were studying the Scriptures; not all were members of the church. The signal went up that housekeeping was necessary, but it was in second place. More important, laypeople were becoming scripturally literate. They were eager for more study. They were receptive to teaching classes, guiding home groups, and providing key leadership. They began to visualize themselves in ministry.[24]

Wilke concludes his reminiscence with this:

If I were to again enter the parish ministry next Sunday morning, the first thing I would do would be to select twenty or thirty gifted laypersons and I would meet with them once a week to train them to be special spiritual leaders in the life of the church. The fire of the gospel will burn when the entire people of God is energized.[25]

There is to be a shared pastoral leadership, and its task is to equip the believers.

21. *Every Christian is a minister.*

By now, this has become clear. The job of the pastors is not to do *all* the work of ministry. Their job is to prepare each Christian to discover and use his spiritual gifts (Eph. 4:11, 12).

Further, the pastor will never be able to know all the people church members know. He will never be able to talk to them about serious things the way their friends can. And he is not gifted to do all the things members can (though perhaps he can do other things). Paul said (1 Cor. 12) that the church is like a body, in which *all* the parts are essential.

You aren't to be a spectator who comes to church and watches the professionals up front. If your church encourages or allows this, something is wrong. Your church should be a place where you worship with others, are nurtured by and help to nurture others, discover and develop your spiritual gifts, and find places of and encouragement in service.

22. *"By their budgets ye shall know them."*

I've always been intrigued by hearing parents or politicians say "We can't afford that." In some cases there is very little money available, just enough for the bare necessities. Often, however, the truth is that money is spent on things that we choose, with the result that there is none left for things others choose.

This is true of church life too. Churches have money and spend it on certain things. They then have no money to spend on other things. When I hear pastors or congregations say, "We'd like to help the poor;" or, "We'd like to help a struggling congregation get on its feet," but "We just can't afford it," I know that it usually means that the church is spending nearly all its money on itself. Thus it really *can't* help anyone else. The point: if you want to know what's important to a family or a congregation, look to see where the money is spent. In the average church, most of the money is spent on itself.

In my denomination (Southern Baptist Convention) in 1985, the average church gave 3.2 percent of its total receipts to SBC causes through our centralized budget, the Cooperative Program.[26] Three and two-tenths! Granted, many churches take other special offerings for foreign, home, and state missions, but the percentage is not changed significantly. In the average Southern Baptist Church, then, around 90 percent of budget receipts are spent *by the congregation on itself!* What is important to us? Look at where we spend our money. We Southern Baptists talk *ad infinitum* about the importance of missions, but we spend 90 percent of our money on ourselves and gave in 1985, per capita, $42.15 to missions.[27] Our SBC *total* giving, per capita for 1985, was $251.15.[28] In other words, five dollars a week.

In the congregation where I worshiped a few years ago, the proposed budget for the next year was distributed for discussion and adoption. Though it was divided into sections (Pastoral Ministry, Education, World Mission, Benevolence, and so forth), there were no percentage figures attached, just total dollar amounts. When I asked (in an open business meeting) for percentages, no one on the budget committee had thought of preparing a figure. When the chairman—on the spot—calculated the percentages, the congregation was surprised to learn that 63 percent of the budget would be spent on staff salaries.

I'm not against staff ministers being paid a good wage. I'm not particularly against big, pretty buildings. What I am against is selfishness which denies the gospel that we

say we believe. We will stand before God someday to jus-
tify our ten thousand dollar chandeliers and fantastic pastors' salaries when we could not send more missionaries
or help the needy "because we don't have the money."

What is important to a congregation? Look to see where
the money is spent. "By their budgets ye shall know them."

For the Church to rise from the ashes into new life, we
must be firmly guided by these principles.

The Shape of the Renewed Church
An Historical Overview

When I was young, I was an avid baseball player and played every season throughout high school. My father, who had been a well-known semipro player in our area, was always our coach. He taught me a lot about the techniques and strategy of baseball, and we often talked about it. But there were some things that couldn't be taught just by words. I didn't profit much from his saying, "On a double play, the shortstop should drag his left foot across the base as he receives the throw." It helped a lot more to throw a couch pillow on the floor and watch as he demonstrated the proper technique.

That is true in church life, too. It doesn't do enough just to say "Your church should nurture believers"; or "Worship should be directed toward God." We need to see congregations and movements who are struggling to rise from the ashes. This chapter will show how some groups, both old and modern, have done it.

Historical Models

Throughout history there have been groups who have tried to form a radically biblical church. Their insights need to be regained today.

Hippolytus

A model of serious discipleship from the third century is found in *The Apostolic Tradition*, written by Hippolytus about A.D. 200.[1] It describes church practice in Rome.

An inquirer, one interested in Christianity (a "seeker"), would have a discussion with the church leaders. Here the gospel was clearly explained and the reality and depth of the inquirer's commitment was determined. This was to protect the integrity of membership, that is, to insure that the new church member knew what Christianity was and what he was getting into. If his faith was considered genuine, he would be brought into the church's life through a ritual called "the rite of welcome." It included a verbal and symbolic rejection of the devil and his works and a verbal and symbolic expression of turning to Christ.

There then followed a period of instruction (the catechumenate), which included teaching and discipling: it normally lasted three years. The emphasis was not so much on learning facts but on learning to walk with Christ—on what moral living means. It was personal, relevant, and "real-life." Correct doctrine was taught to counter the prevalent heresy of the day. This basic training in Christian truth was essential: there is one God; Jesus is God; he was born of the Holy Spirit and the Virgin Mary, and so forth.

At the end of this long, intense period of instruction in doctrine and right living, the converting person went through the rite of election, a service that symbolized God choosing the person and the person's choosing God.

There finally came a six-week period of serious spiritual preparation for baptism ("purification and enlightenment"). It included intensive Scripture study, prayer, and fasting, and was usually conducted during Lent. It ended on Easter Sunday, when the convert was baptized. The Church's sacraments were then received for the first time. After baptism came a follow-up period of further teaching. Until A.D. 400, nearly all baptismal candidates were adults.[2]

Anabaptism

Another model of Church renewal and serious discipleship is the Anabaptist ("re-baptizer") movement. Amid the ferment of the Reformation, the Anabaptists began in Zurich, Switzerland, in 1525. A group of young men (including Conrad Grebel, Felix Manz, and Georg Blaurock) in frustration broke away from what they considered the compromising reforms of Ulrich Zwingli in Zurich.

The Anabaptists (who called themselves "the Brethren") emphasized the authority of Scripture alone (particularly the New Testament), the necessity of conversion and personal faith, the Church as composed of believers only (as a "gathered church," opposed to the territorial churches of the Roman Catholics, Luther, Zwingli, and Calvin), baptism of believers only, strict church discipline, religious liberty, and (in most cases) withdrawal from social life (such as government service, and military service).

The Anabaptists spread into several wings. Modern-day Mennonites, Church of the Brethren, Moravians, and Hutterians are direct descendants of the sixteenth-century movement. Baptist groups, while not lineally descended from the Anabaptists, are their kin in theology and ethos.

All Anabaptist groups practiced serious discipleship. Rejecting traditional structures and beliefs, they were persecuted across Europe by both Roman Catholics and Protestants. They separated from "worldliness," lived a simple life, and emphasized love and forbearance. Serious discipleship was encouraged by a strict church discipline that required ethical living of those claiming to be the Lord's people. Some groups, notably the Hutterians, carried this pattern of intense Christian life all the way to the practice of community of gods.[3]

A fascinating modern expression of radical Christian life is seen in the over 260 Hutterian *Bruderhofs* (communities) in America and Canada. One such community was begun in Germany in 1920 by Eberhard and Emmy Arnold. In

1930 it united with the Hutterian Church. Following years of Nazi persecution, the group was expelled from Germany in 1937 and fled to England. Facing internment after World War II began, the community emigrated in 1940-41 to Paraguay. In 1954 a branch community began in the USA, and in 1961 the whole group arrived from Paraguay. There are now three communities in the USA (Woodcrest, Rifton, NY; New Meadow Run, Farmington, PA; Deer Spring, Norfolk, CT.) and one in England (Darvell, Robertsbridge, East Sussex).[4]

Pietism

Another of these models is a German Lutheran movement of the seventeenth and eighteenth centuries called Pietism.[5] It was a reaction to the cold orthodoxy of the late sixteenth century.

A hundred years after Luther's death (that is, by 1650) Europe was devastated from the Thirty Year's War (1618-1648). Even in the Lutheran territories of northern Germany, the princes ruled in religious matters. Further, Lutheran theology had sunk to a period of intense scrutiny of minutiae as it defined itself against the various theological positions that had come from the Reformation: Roman Catholic, Calvinist, Anglican, Anabaptist. In this Protestant Scholasticism, concern for heart-religion had not been totally lost, but the emphasis was clearly on orthodox theology. To use an oft-remodeled phrase, Luther was much revered but little known. The churches, in the main, became cool, intellectual, and devoid of spiritual life.

There were voices of protest, the most prominent being Lutheran pastor Johann Arndt (1555-1621). His 1605 book *Wahres Christenthum (True Christianity)* was a lament over the sad state of Lutheranism and a call for reform of church life. "True Christianity," he wrote, "consists namely in the exhibition of a true, living, and active faith which manifests itself in genuine godliness and the fruits of righteousness."[6]

Arndt's work was of great influence on Philip Jakob Spener (1635-1705). A brilliant boy, heavily influenced by his
devoted Christian mother, Spener received his master's degree at age eighteen. After receiving his doctor of theology
degree from the University of Strassburg, he was ordained
into the Lutheran ministry and took up an important post
as senior pastor at Frankfurt-am-Main in 1666. He became
increasingly disinterested in academic theology; his concern was practical life and faith, and how theology and the
church fit into it. His views were clearly set out in 1675,
when his preface to a new edition of Arndt's work was
published separately as *Pia Desideria* (*Earnest Desires for the
True Reform of the Evangelical Church*). Spener is the father
of Pietism and his book is its central statement. The emphasis on new birth, spiritual life, and the priesthood of
believers (including every-member ministry) spread widely
both in the church and outside.

As early as 1669 Spener had come to see that the church's
identity required that Christians meet together regularly in
small groups to encourage and discipline one another. This
was not, to Spener, a pastoral strategy but a necessary cor-
relate of ecclesiology. In part, he said

> It is certain in any case, that we preachers cannot instruct the
> people from our pulpits as much as is needful unless other per-
> sons in the congregation who by God's grace have a superior
> knowledge of Christianity, take pains by virtue of their universal
> Christian priesthood, to work with and under us to correct and
> reform as much in their neighbours as they are able according to
> the measure of their gifts and their simplicity.[7]

The next year, 1670, Spener actually established meetings
to provide this mutual encouragement and oversight. Luther and Martin Butzer had both suggested such small
groups, though there is no evidence that either ever actually
started them. Further, Jean de Labadie and Jakob Boehme
had instituted house meetings in Geneva and Gorlitz, re-
spectively. These movements were so small and short-lived,

however, that Spener must be credited with discovering a
crucial biblical motif.[8]

The groups, called *Collegia pietatis* (pious gatherings),
grew from a Sunday-afternoon class held in Spener's home.
At church members' request, Spener in 1670 began a pri-
vate home meeting for mutual ministry and growth. Meeting twice weekly and attended by both men and women
(though women were seated separately and not encouraged
to speak), the group at first discussed the previous Sunday's
sermon or read devotional works. Later, Scripture became
the focus of discussion.

Spener was, as Derksen says, "advising tutorial groups
in piety."[9] The danger of dissension was clearly seen. In
Pia Desideria he wrote five years later

> Everything should be arranged with an eye to the glory of God,
> to the spiritual growth of the participants, and therefore also their
> limitations. Any threat of meddlesomeness, quarrelsomeness, self-
> seeking, . . . or something else of this sort should be guarded
> against and tactfully cut off especially by the preachers who retain
> leadership in these meetings.[10]

In these groups, the pietists hoped, there would be support in the struggle against sin and growth in godliness.

The purpose of the groups was to renew the greater *ecclesia*, Church. If the entire Church was to be renewed, a
start must be made with those serious Christians in each
congregation. These *ecclesiolae in ecclesia* ("little churches
within the Church") were not intended, however, to replace
the institutional church. They were to function as a leaven
whose influence would permeate the whole lump. Accord-
ingly, Spener forbade celebration of the sacraments in the
home groups; they were for the entire congregation only.
The groups, furthermore, were not to consider themselves
to be the "real" Church as opposed to the institutional one.
In *Pia Desideria* Spener wrote that the *Collegia* were to be

> Instrumentalities through which the Church was to be brought
> again to reflect the image of the early Christian community. . . .

[They] were not meant to be the means to separate "true" Christians from others and of imbuing the former with a pharisaical self-image.[11]

Results, however, did not measure up to expectations. Though thousands were helped, the full reformation of the Church in Germany did not emerge. In Frankfurt, a suspicious city council ordered the groups to meet in the church building rather than in homes. This, Spener, reported, caused the people to cease speaking openly in the meeting; it was, in fact, its death knell. Further, some *Collegia* did break away from the church and form separatist congregations, which were bitterly critical of the established Church. Spener's biographer suspects that this came from Spener's indecisive direction and his unwillingness to stop dangerous developments.[12] Indeed, by 1703 (thirty-three years after the beginning of the *Collegia*, Spener had become cynical and cautious about the groups and established no others when he moved from Frankfurt. Finally, Pietism in Germany faced two formidable foes. First, their extreme emphasis on "life" led to a too-subjective position; they did not adequately emphasize doctrine. Second, the resistance of the established, institutional Lutheran church (with governmental backing) could not be overcome. The resulting despair led to acquiescence or separation.[13]

The Moravian Brethren

The Church called the Moravian Brethren has a long, complex history.[14] Tracing their roots to the followers of John Hus (1372?-1415) and molded by Peter Chelcicky (1390?-1460?), the Moravians were reorganized by Count Nicholas von Zinzendorf (1700-1760) in 1727 and called the Renewed Moravian church. This new movement fused the vibrant spirit of Pietism (familiar to Zinzendorf) with the old stream of Hussite history and practice.[15] It was Moravians in England who decisively influenced John Wesley spiritually and, though he would eventually break with them, the Moravians contributed heavily to Wesley's methods for church renewal.

Zinzendorf did not intend for the Moravians to become a separate church. Like Spener's Pietist groups, the Moravian communities were to be *ecclesiolae in ecclesia* (little churches within the Church) whose purpose was to renew the whole Church.[16] People should remain in their own denomination but participate in addition in a more disciplined community. Though few in number, the Moravians gave to the church-renewal movement the techniques of society, class, and band.

English Religious Societies

The idea of small, disciplined groups of Christians spread from Germany to England. Anthony Horneck, a well-known Anglican preacher, left the Continent for England in 1661 and in 1678 (eight years after Spener's first group) began to organize small groups (or societies) of Anglicans for instruction, encouragement, and discipline. These Anglican religious societies spread rapidly; in the early 1700s at least forty such groups were functioning in London.[17] For its part, the Anglican leadership permitted and encouraged the societies.

Samuel Wesley, Anglican rector at Epworth and father of John and Charles Wesley, founded such a small group or society in his parish in 1702. The three purposes of the society, he wrote, were: to pray, to read the Scriptures and discuss spiritual matters for the spiritual benefit of the members, and to discuss and implement ways to help the needy. These societies, Samuel Wesley concluded, provided the benefits of medieval monasticism without its inconveniences.[18] Further, during her husband Samuel's prolonged absence in 1712, his wife Susanna Wesley formed a small group society in their home and to great effect. It is no surprise that their children, John and Charles, formed a similar society during their Oxford days, which was called the "Holy Club" and whose members were mockingly jeered as "Methodists" because of their strict spiritual disciplines.

The Wesleyan Movement

The story of the Wesleys' ordination into the Anglican ministry, their failed mission work in Georgia, John's despair and return home, and his conversion in 1738 through the influence of the Moravians in London is well known. With the Moravian band-organizer Peter Böhler, the Wesleys in 1738 formed a new society which met in Fetter Lane in London. John Wesley even visited Zinzendorf's estate, Herrnhut, in Germany. Within two years, however, Wesley had broken with his Moravian mentors over their quietism, their emphasis on Zinzendorf, and their tendency to be spiritually complacent.[19] Further, in 1739 John had joined his friend George Whitefield in field preaching to the poor in Bristol, a hundred miles from London. The response was amazing! Hundreds were convicted of their sin and deeply interested in the gospel.

The question that now faced Wesley was what to do with the hundreds of converts. The answer was obvious: he quickly began organizing them into societies and bands and he soon bought a piece of property to provide a central meeting place. He spent time in London and Bristol, preaching in the open air, speaking to societies, and organizing bands. When the societies grew too large for his personal care, he selected helpers who had gifts for preaching and pastoral care of the converts, and he began holding annual conferences for these leaders.[20]

As the numbers of converts grew, Wesley saw that he could not visit each one personally each week. In London they began to meet together on Thursday night, Wesley promising to "spend some time with you in prayer, and give you the best advice I can."[21] Without intention or plan, then, there arose what came to be called the Methodist societies. Prospective members had to meet only one entrance requirement: "a desire to flee from the wrath to come, to be saved from their sins."[22] Their purpose, Wesley said, was "to pray together, to receive the word of exhortation, and to watch over one another in love, that they might help each other to work out their salvation."[23] In town after town, new Methodist societies were born. Wesley often spoke to preexisting societies, as well.

Late in 1738, Wesley had drawn up rules for bands. Based upon the Moravian model, these were small groups of around six members, men and women in separate groups, who met weekly for confession of sin and pastoral care. Only people assured of salvation could join and only those who desired a deeper, more intimate fellowship. They were expected to avoid known sin, do good works (including giving to the poor), and make use of the means of grace (such as, worship, reception of the sacraments, fellowship, prayer, Scripture study, and so forth). Four questions were asked each week of each member: What known sins have you committed since the last meeting? What temptations have you met with? How were you delivered? And what have you thought, said, or done which may or may not be sin? Snyder estimates that perhaps only 20 percent of Methodist people met in bands.[24]

By 1742, however, Wesley faced another problem: many Methodists did not live the gospel. They fell away from their initial commitment and lapsed into sin. Some system was required for exercising discipline. The Bristol society, now numbering eleven hundred, was divided into classes of about twelve people which met weekly. Wesley appointed leaders for each class, who received a weekly offering for the debt on the preaching house, and inquired into the behavior of the class members. They regularly reported to the ministers of the society on the health and spiritual condition of the members. The method was soon introduced in London and elsewhere. The result, Wesley said, was that:

> . . . Evil men were detected, and reproved. They were borne with for a season. If they forsook their sins, we received them gladly; if they obstinately persisted therein, it was openly declared that they were not of us. The rest mourned and prayed for them, and

yet rejoiced, that, as far as in us lay, the scandal was rolled away from the society.[25]

Wesley was ecstatic about the result of this new structure for discipline and admonition:

> It can scarce be conceived what advantages have been reaped from this little prudential regulation. Many now happily experienced that Christian fellowship of which they had not so much as an idea before. They began to "bear one another's burdens," and naturally to "care for each other." As they had daily a more intimate acquaintance with, so they had a more endeared affection for, each other. And, "speaking the truth in love, they grew up into Him in all things, who is the Head, even Christ."[26]

Though the classes stimulated fellowship and spiritual growth, their basic purpose was to provide discipline. Before one could join the society, one had to join a class. To put it another way, one could not be part of the large group unless one submitted to the discipline of the small group. Only faithful class members received admission tickets to the quarterly society love feast. Snyder remarks that the classes were the cornerstone of the entire Methodist system. "They were in effect house churches (not classes for instruction, as the term *class* might suggest), meeting in the various neighborhoods where people lived. . . ."[27]

The classes served as an evangelistic tool (most of the conversions occurred in this context) and as a discipling agent. The class leaders, who were more mature Christians, were in fact (if not in name) pastors of their flock. Wesley believed that spiritual oversight must be personal, based on a deep relationship with the people. In the classes, further, there was plural leadership, that is, more than one leader. Spiritual oversight was shared.

The classes and bands were overseen by traveling lay preachers appointed by Wesley and under his direct supervision.

Wesley's vision was to create within the Church of England a real people of God, *ecclesiolae in ecclesia*. These

Methodists were to renew the Church at large. And the way Wesley planned to do this was by focusing not on leading a person *to* a decision for Christ, but on what happened *after* the decision.[28] As Snyder concludes,

> . . . Wesley saw the world as his parish, but he "refused to preach in any place where he could not follow it up by organized Societies with adequate leadership." He was out to make disciples— disciples who would renew the whole church.[29]

And did it work? From its beginning in 1738, Wesley's movement grew dramatically:

after thirty years (1768), there were forty circuits with 27,341 members;

after forty years (1778), there were sixty circuits with 40,089 members;

after fifty years (1788), there were 99 circuits with 66,375 members;

after sixty years (1798), there were 149 circuits with 101,712 members.[30]

This averages about one Methodist for every thirty Englishmen! All this from a single man who saw the real church to be a body of people who confessed Christ and watched over one another in love and who were helped by others who were more mature, who were in turn overseen by others.

Modern Models

Space limitations prohibit detailing here the many examples of churches who are implementing God's ways. But they do exist, and God is blessing them! New life is flourishing amid the ashes.

The 1920s-1930s model of Episcopalian Sam Shoemaker can be studied with good result,[31] as well as the 1940s-1960s

Church of the Savior in Washington, D.C.[32] Southern Baptist pastor David Haney relates his attempts at leading a Maryland church into renewal,[33] while Robert Girard describes efforts with a Wesleyan church in Arizona.[34] Lawrence Richards discusses three churches in renewal in various parts of the country.[35] Ralph Neighbour, Jr., describes renewal efforts in a Southern Baptist congregation in Houston,[36] while Graham Pulkingham relives the metamorphosis of an Episcopal congregation in the same city.[37] Michael Green, then rector of St. Aldate's Church (Anglican) in Oxford, England, has described his work in a parish,[38] while an Anglican diocese's experiments in renewal are described in Stephen Verney's book.[39] Paul Cho's efforts in Korea can be examined,[40] and other resources can be pursued further.[41]

6

First Steps
Get Started!

A ll this theory is fine," I hear you saying, "but how do we do it?" That, I think, will depend on your situation. But there are some beginning steps.

Step One

First, understand the ideas and principles we've discussed here. To have a chance of success, you must clearly understand what should be done, what can be done, and where you're trying to go. Don't rush in where cautious pastors fear to tread. Take some time. Read other books (such as those which I have included in the Notes and Bibliography). Find a kindred spirit (church member or fellow Christian from outside your congregation) and talk about these issues. Pray for understanding and insight.

Step Two

Second, preach and teach about these ideas. We can't expect people to leave old, established patterns for new ones if we haven't informed them. In the church where I served, I

preached for five Sundays on the tasks of the Church,
spending a Sunday morning and evening sermon on each.
Some Sunday nights, when it fit, I reserved part of the
sermon time for the congregation's responses to what I'd
suggested in the sermons.

I believe that what I've suggested is biblical, but it isn't
what many of our people have heard. So teach them from
the Word of God what God expects of us. Start expressing
some of these ideas in committee meetings (for example
when someone suggests adding another unnecessary program to an already overburdened schedule). Gradually let
people begin to think along with you.

Step Three

Third, start. It may not be proper for your congregation
to jump in headfirst on all these ideas. You must determine
that. But when you have clearly understood what you want
to do, and when you've taught your people about it, then
start and do something! Inertia is our greatest enemy.

For example, after you've done some reading and thinking to better understand worship, teach the congregation
about it. Then *put into practice* something of what you've
learned and taught. Deepen the worship. Turn the spotlight
away from men and onto God.

In the church where I served, we set out to do this. I
eschewed "hot-dogging" in the worship service and gently
encouraged other worship leaders to do the same. We involved more lay people in the worship so that the preacher
wasn't up front putting on the show; worship was an *act
of the people*. Ushers helped to welcome people as they
arrived. One of our young spiritual leaders (a member of
the pastoral team that was emerging) welcomed the people
and the guests; he had a gift for making visitors feel at
home. Members stood and greeted one another and the
guests with genuine warmth. A layman led the singing.
We had three readings from Scripture each Sunday morn-

ing, and three different laypersons each week (asked beforehand) simply stood where they were and read aloud the Word of God. The prayer time was guided, but with long stretches of silence so the people could pray instead of listening to someone else pray. We tried, I'm saying, to structure worship so that it was an offering of the congregation to God rather than a show put on by the preacher. We followed a very simple pattern:

Lord, Hear Our Praise

Welcome and announcements

Hymn(s) or more modern praise choruses

The prayers of the people

Hymn(s)

The offering

Lord, Teach Us Your Ways

The Scripture readings

Special music (often omitted—we didn't have great musicians)

The sermon

The hymn of commitment

The benediction

What we did with worship was not earthshaking or fancy or trendy. We simply tried, in our situation, to put into practice the truth that worship is praise to God rather than entertainment. We started.

For example, in regard to nurture, make a beginning. Start small if you need to. Invite two or three people to start having breakfast or lunch once a week and start nurturing them. Draw others in. Then let them start nurturing. Or start a small group meeting in someone's home. In our little church, the Wednesday-night-prayer meeting crowd *was* a small group—we had twelve or fifteen come. Over a few months' time, I moved them out of the sanctuary and into the fellowship hall. Instead of sitting in pews we sat in a circle. I planned for the first ten minutes to be "talk time." I let them just talk, enjoying the fellowship with each other. Then I would start focusing; I would ask someone how he or she was doing this week; then I'd ask someone else. I was teaching them how to talk openly, in a nonthreatening setting, about real-life, personal things. I would have a brief (twenty-minute) Bible study, with emphasis on asking questions to get them to talk and apply it to their lives. We would finish with prayer requests and prayer. Occasionally I would change the whole thing and have people break up into groups of four to six and go around the circle answering questions that I had prepared (such as, "tell us about how you met Christ"; or "tell about a time when you felt especially close to God"; or "what are you happy about tonight?"; or "what are you concerned about tonight?"). I was trying to stimulate personal knowledge of each other and thus personal concern for each other. And they loved it!

In regard to ruthlessly evaluating, find who to share it with and start doing it. Maybe part of each deacons' meeting (or church council, or whatever you decide) could be given to asking "How are we doing in the Lord's work here? Given the five tasks, how's it going?" Or maybe hold a planning/evaluation retreat with church leaders. I preached an annual "State of the Church" sermon in which I gave my impressions of how we are doing. But, however you do it, start and do it!

Conclusion
Up From the Ashes

Will the Church of Jesus rise from the ashes of institutionalism, bureaucratization, and arrogant denominationalism? Will secular ideologies continue to control various wings of the Church? Will we continue to argue about irrelevant, secondary points of theology while we, in our living, deny the basic truths of our faith? Will we continue blindly on, building our earthly empires that the world increasingly ignores as irrelevant? Can we escape the cultural captivity that strangles the life out of us and robs us of our power? The Church must repent or face judgment. Our pride must go. Our hearts and minds must open as wide as God's promises. We must be prepared to suffer and be misunderstood.

Thoughtful Christians have written movingly of "the renewing church," a church emerging from the smoldering ashes.[1] Bloesch notes:

> The age of denominations is coming to an end. Provincialism and insularism are being superseded by the need for a unified Christian witness against the principalities and powers of our time. A one-world church, however, is not the answer to the problem of Christian disunity, since it in effect substitutes or-

ganizational strategy, even technological efficiency, for trust in the divine initiative and obedience to the divine imperative.

What we should strive for is a faith that is more conservative than conservative Protestantism, more catholic than Roman Catholicism, and more radical than liberal Protestantism and avantgarde Catholicism. By returning to the biblical roots of our faith we can recover the catholicity of vision that the church needs in our time as well as a renewed appreciation for the historical heritage that conserves and maintains this heritage.[2]

Webber adds:

The renewing church is the church in quest of a more dynamic faith, a faith that has shifted away from the old debates between Christian groups. Instead, the renewing church seeks unity, spirituality, worship, and involvement in the lives of other people.[3]

This is the Church that must emerge from the ashes. This is the Church of Jesus, stripped of all hypocrisy, triumphalism, and arrogance. This is the Church of Jesus, freed from cultural captivity, institutionalism, and the chauvinism of the present. This is real, radical Christianity.

Here am I, Lord. Send me.

Source Notes

Introduction

1. David Watson, *Called and Committed: World-Changing Discipleship* (Wheaton: Shaw, 1982), preface.

2. Howard Snyder, *The Radical Wesley: Pattern for Church Renewal* (Grand Rapids: Zondervan, 1987), preface.

3. Donald Bloesch, *Crumbling Foundations* (Grand Rapids: Zondervan, 1984), p. 15. This prophetic book should be widely read.

4. Ibid., p. 29.

5. Ibid., p. 91.

6. These figures are reported by Bloesch, pp. 83-85.

7. Bloesch, p. 85. Also "North American Scene," *Christianity Today* (8 August 1986).

8. Bloesch, p. 85.

9. Ibid., pp. 84, 52.

10. "The Win Arn Church Growth Report," no. 19 (1987), p. 1.

11. "1986 'Stagnant' for SBC," *Baptist Standard,* (18 February 1987), p. 5. Also Avery Willis, Jr., "Plugging the Leak in the Baptistry," *The Commission* (September 1987), p. 79.

12. "Missions Memo," *Missions USA* (May-June 1987), p. 4.

13. Bloesch, *Crumbling Foundations*, pp. 23, 52.

14. Ibid., pp. 15, 84.

Chapter 2   Who Are We?

1. Robert Webber, *Evangelicals on the Canterbury Trail* (Waco: Word, 1985), p. 58.

2. Resources for a scholarly study of the Church's nature are legion. Some suggestions are R. Newton Flew, *Jesus and His Church* (London: Epworth, 1960), Rudolf Schnackenburg, *The Church in the New Testament*, tr. W. J. O'Hara (New York: Herder and Herder, 1965), Paul S. Minear, *Images of the Church in the New Testament* (Philadelphia: Westminster, 1960), and C. K. Barrett, *Church, Ministry, and Sacraments in the New Testament* (Grand Rapids: Eerdmans, 1985). Articles abound in journals and the standard theological dictionaries. A more applicational approach is in Michael Green's books, *Called to Serve* (Philadelphia: Westminster, 1964) and *Freed to Serve* (London: Hodder and Stoughton, 1983).

Chapter 3   What Are We Doing Here?

1. C. H. Dodd, *The Apostolic Preaching and Its Developments* (New York: Willette Clark & Co., 1937), pp. 25–29.

2. C. Peter Wagner, *Your Church Can Grow* (Glendale, CA: Regal Books, 1977), pp. 76–78.

3. Wayne Rood, *On Nurturing Christians* (Nashville: Abingdon, 1972), p. 60.

4. See Elizabeth O'Connor, *Call to Commitment* (New York: Harper & Row, 1976, pp. 23–38.

5. Gene Getz, *Sharpening the Focus of the Church* (Chicago: Moody, 1974), p. 202. On the faulty "schooling-instructional" paradigm, see John H. Westerhoff, *Will Our Children Have Faith?* (New York: Harper & Row, 1983), p. 6.

6. William H. Willimon, "Making Christians in a Secular World," *Christian Century* (22 October 1986): p. 916.

7. For more resources, see Ronald H. Nash, ed., *Evangelical Renewal in the Mainline Denominations* (Westchester, IL: Crossway Books, 1987).

8. For another approach, see Jon Johnston, *Christian Excellence: An Alternative to Success* (Grand Rapids: Baker, 1985).

Chapter 4   Principles that Shape Church Life

1. Maegorzata Niezabitowski, *Remnants: The Last Jews in Poland* tr. William Brand and Hanna Dobosiewicz (Friendly Press, 1986). Cited in *National Geographic* 170 (September 1986), p. 379.

2. M. Scott Peck, *The Road Less Travelled* (New York: Simon and Schuster, 1978), p. 24.

3. Ibid., p. 26.

4. Gary Smalley and John Trent, *The Blessing* (Nashville: Thomas Nelson, 1986), pp. 143–6.

5. Michael Green in "St. Aldate's International Linkletter," March 1984.

6. Quoted by Frank B. Minirth and Paul D. Meier in *Happiness Is a Choice: A Manual on the Symptoms, Causes, and Cures of Depression* (Grand Rapids: Baker, 1978), p. 7.

7. Erik Erikson, *Childhood and Society,* 2nd ed. (New York: Norton, 1963); *Identity, Youth, and Crisis* (New York: Norton, 1968); *Insight and Responsibility* (New York: Norton, 1964). Also see Robert Coles, *Erik H. Erikson: The Growth of His Work* (Jersey City, NJ: Da Capo, 1987).

8. Daniel Levinson, et. al. *The Seasons of a Man's Life* (New York: Knopf, 1978).

9. James W. Fowler, *Stages of Faith* (San Francisco: Harper and Row, 1981).

10. Linda Lawson, "Some Outreach Methods Ineffective," *Facts and Trends* (Nashville: Baptist Sunday School Board), April 1987, p. 3.

11. Warren J. Hartman, "Five Audiences," *Discipleship Trends* (Nashville: The General Board of Discipleship of the United Methodist Church), October 1983. Vol I: no. 1, pp. 1–4.

12. Ibid., p. 4.

13. Linda Lawson, "Potential Exists for Conflict," *Facts and Trends* (Nashville: Baptist Sunday School Board), May 1987, p. 3.

14. For example: J. W. MacGorman, *The Gifts of the Spirit* (Nashville: Broadman, 1980), Ralph Neighbour, Jr., *This Gift Is Mine* (Nashville: Broadman Films, 1976), Peter Wagner, *Your Spiritual Gifts Can Help Your Church Grow* (Glendale, CA: Regal, 1979).

15. Robert C. Girard, *Brethren, Hang Loose! Or What's Happening to My Church?* (Grand Rapids: Zondervan, 1972), pp. 27, 28.

16. Ibid., p. 73.

17. Ralph Neighbour, Jr., *The Seven Last Words of the Church* (Nashville: Broadman, 1979), p. 16.

18. Richard B. Wilke, *And Are We Yet Alive? The Future of the United Methodist Church* (Nashville: Abingdon, 1986), p. 47.

19. Ibid., p. 33.

20. Clayton Sullivan, *Called to Preach, Condemned to Survive: The Education of Clayton Sullivan* (Macon, GA: Mercer, 1985), pp. 167, 168.

21. Wilke, *And Are We Yet Alive?* p. 100.

22. Michael Green, *Freed to Serve* (London: Hodder and Stoughton, 1983), pp. 10–16.

23. Elton Trueblood, *The Company of the Committed* (New York: Harper & Row, 1980), p. 63.

24. Wilke, *And Are We Yet Alive?* pp. 119, 120. The Lutherans have

developed St. Stephen Ministries, which provides a year's training in caring for the ill, the elderly, shut-ins, those in grief, and divorced persons. Wilke has prepared a series, *Disciple: Becoming Disciples Through Bible Study* (Cokesbury, forthcoming). Most major denominations have or are developing similar programs, for instance, Southern Baptists' *Masterlife* or the Roman Catholic Church's *Cursillo* and *Renew.* For more examples, see Ronald H. Nash, ed., *Evangelical Renewal in the Mainline Churches* (Westchester, IL: Crossway Books, 1987).

25. Wilke, *And Are We Yet Alive?* p. 120.

26. "Southern Baptist Highlights," *The Quarterly Review.* July-September 1986: p. 55.

27. Ibid., p. 48.

28. Ibid., p. 49.

Chapter 5   The Shape of the Renewed Church

1. See Robert Webber's discussion in *The Majestic Tapestry* (Nashville: Thomas Nelson, 1986), pp. 149–161.

2. J. N. Hillgarth, ed. *The Conversion of Western Europe, 350–750* (Englewood Cliffs, NJ: Prentice-Hall, 1969), p. 9.

3. On the radical Christianity of the Anabaptists, see William R. Estep, *The Anabaptist Story* (Grand Rapids: Eerdmans, 1975) and Donald F. Durnbaugh, *The Believer's Church: The History and Character of Radical Protestantism* (Scottsdale, PA: Herald Press, 1968).

4. On the Eberhard Arnold *Bruderhof,* see Emmy Arnold, *Torches Together* (Rifton, NY: Plough, 1964). Several books by and about Eberhard Arnold, along with a quarterly journal (*The Plough*) are available from the Hutterian Society of Brothers, Rt. 213, Rifton, NY 12471.

5. This discussion relies heavily on Kenneth J. Derksen's excellent article "The *Collegium Pietatis* as a Model for Home Bible Study Groups," *Crux* XXII, no. 4 (December 1986): pp. 16–26. See also Donald F. Durnbaugh, *The Believers' Church: the History and Character of Radical Protestantism.*

6. Derksen, "The *Collegium Pietatis*," p. 17.

7. Ibid., p. 20.

8. Ibid., p. 21.

9. Ibid., p. 22.

10. Ibid., pp. 21, 22.

11. Ibid., p. 24.

12. Ibid., p. 22.

13. Ibid., p. 24.

14. A good overview is in Durnbaugh, *The Believers' Church*, pp. 51–63.

15. Ibid., p. 63.

16. Howard A. Snyder, *The Radical Wesley: Pattern for Church Renewal* (Grand Rapids: Zondervan, 1987), pp. 24, 27. This excellent book is "required reading" for people serious about renewal. It is based on the author's doctoral dissertation at the University of Notre Dame, *Pietism, Moravianism, and Methodism as Renewal Movements: A Comparative and Thematic Study* (Ann Arbor: University Microfilms, 1983).

17. Snyder, *The Radical Wesley*, p. 15.

18. Ibid., pp. 15, 16.

19. Ibid., pp. 27–30.

20. Ibid., pp. 29–34.

21. Ibid., p. 34.

22. Ibid., p. 35.

23. Ibid., p. 34.

24. Ibid., p. 60.

25. Ibid., pp. 36, 37.

26. Ibid., p. 37.

27. Ibid., p. 54.

28. Ibid., p. 2.

29. Ibid., p. 64.

30. Ibid., p. 54.

31. Irving Harris, *The Breeze of the Spirit* (New York: Seabury, 1978).

32. Elizabeth O'Connor, *Call to Commitment* (New York: Harper & Row, 1976) and *Journey Inward, Journey Outward* (New York: Harper & Row, 1975).

33. David Haney, *Renew My Church* (Grand Rapids: Zondervan, 1972), *The Idea of the Laity* (Grand Rapids: Zondervan, 1973), and *Breakthrough Into Renewal* (Nashville: Broadman, 1974).

34. Robert C. Girard, *Brethren, Hang Loose!* (Grand Rapids: Zondervan, 1972).

35. Lawrence O. Richards, *Three Churches in Renewal* (Grand Rapids: Zondervan, 1975).

36. Ralph Neighbour, Jr., *The Seven Last Words of the Church* (Nashville: Broadman, 1979).

37. Graham Pulkingham, "A Church Reborn," in *The Spirit and The Church*, comp. Ralph Martin (New York: Paulist, 1976). Also Pulkingham, *Gathered for Power* (New York: Morehouse-Barlow, 1972) and *They Left Their Nets* (New York: Morehouse-Barlow, 1973).

38. Michael Green, "The Marks of Authentic Christianity," (Vancouver, B.C.: Regent College, 1980), and in *Freed to Serve* (London:

Hodder and Stoughton, 1983), chapters 9 and 10. The taped lecture is chillingly prophetic.

39. Stephen Verney, *Fire in Coventry* (Westwood, NJ: Revell, 1964).

40. Paul Cho and Harold Hostetler, *Successful Home Cell Groups* (Plainfield, NJ: Logos International, 1981).

41. For example, Gene Getz, *Sharpening the Focus of the Church* (Chicago: Moody, 1974), Howard Snyder, *The Problem of Wineskins: Church Renewal in a Technological Age* (Downer's Grove: Inter-Varsity, 1975), R. Paul Stevens, *Liberating the Laity* (Downer's Grove: Inter-Varsity, 1985), Bernard J. Lee and Michael A. Cowen, *Dangerous Memories: House Churches and Our American Way* (Kansas City, MO: Sheed & Ward, 1986), and C. Kirk Hadaway, Francis M. DuBose, and Stuart A. Wright, *Home Cell Groups and House Churches* (Nashville: Broadman, 1987).

Conclusion

1. See Robert Webber, *The Majestic Tapestry* (Nashville: Thomas Nelson, 1986) and *Evangelicals on the Canterbury Trail* (Waco: Word, 1985).

2. Donald Bloesch, *Crumbling Foundations* (Grand Rapids: Zondervan, 1984), p. 25.

3. Webber, *The Majestic Tapestry* p. 227.

Bibliography

Barrett, C. K. *Church, Ministry, and Sacraments in the New Testament.* Grand Rapids: Eerdmans, 1985.

Bloesch, Donald. *Crumbling Foundations.* Grand Rapids: Zondervan, 1984.

Cho, Paul and Hostetler, Harold. *Successful Home Cell Groups.* Plainfield, NJ: Logos International, 1981.

Claypool, John. *Opening Blind Eyes.* Nashville: Abingdon, 1983.

————— . *The Preaching Event.* Waco: Word, 1980.

————— . *Stages: The Art of Living the Expected.* Waco: Word, 1977.

————— . *Tracks of a Fellow Struggler.* Waco: Word, 1974.

Coles, Robert. *Erik Erikson: The Growth of His Work.* Jersey City: Da Capo, 1987.

Derksen, Kenneth J. "The *Collegium Pietatis* as a Model for Home Bible Study Groups," *Crux* XXII (December 1986): 16–26.

Dodd, C. H. *The Apostolic Preaching and Its Developments.* New York: Willette Clark & Co., 1937.

Durnbaugh, Donald F. *The Believers' Church: the History and Character of Radical Protestantism.* Scottsdale, PA: Herald Press, 1985.

Erikson, Erik H. *Childhood and Society.* 2nd edition. New York: Norton, 1963.

————— . *Identity, Youth, and Crisis.* New York: Norton, 1968.

————— . *Insight and Responsibility.* New York: Norton, 1964.

Flew, R. Newton. *Jesus and His Church*. London: Epworth, 1960.

Foster, Richard. *Celebration of Discipline*. San Francisco: Harper & Row, 1978.

————— . *The Freedom of Simplicity*. San Francisco: Harper & Row, 1981.

Fowler, James W. *Stages of Faith*. San Francisco: Harper & Row, 1981.

Getz, Gene. *Sharpening the Focus of the Church*. Chicago: Moody, 1974.

Girard, Robert C. *Brethren, Hang Loose!* Grand Rapids: Zondervan, 1972.

Green, Michael. *Called to Serve*. Philadelphia: Westminster, 1964.

————— . *Evangelism in the Early Church*. Grand Rapids: Eerdmans, 1970.

————— . *Evangelism, Then and Now*. Downer's Grove, IL: Inter-Varsity Press, 1982.

————— . *Freed to Serve*. London: Hodder and Stoughton, 1983.

Hadaway, C. Kirk; DuBose, Francis M.; and Wright, Stuart A. *Home Cell Groups and House Churches*. Nashville: Broadman, 1987.

Haney, David. *Breakthrough Into Renewal*. Nashville: Broadman, 1974.

————— . *The Idea of the Laity*. Grand Rapids: Zondervan, 1973.

————— . *Renew My Church*. Grand Rapids: Zondervan, 1972.

Harris, Irving. *The Breeze of the Spirit*. New York: Seabury, 1978.

Johnston, Jon. *Christian Excellence: An Alternative to Success*. Grand Rapids: Baker, 1985.

Lee, Bernard J., and Cowen, Michael A. *Dangerous Memories: House Churches and Our American Way*. Kansas City, MO: Sheed & Ward, 1986.

Levinson, Daniel J. *The Seasons of a Man's Life*. New York: Knopf, 1978.

MacGorman, J. W. *The Gifts of the Spirit*. Nashville: Broadman, 1980.

Miller, Keith. *A Second Touch*. Waco: Word, 1982.

————— . *The Taste of New Wine*. Waco: Word, 1982.

Minear, Paul S. *Images of the Church in the New Testament*. Philadelphia: Westminster, 1960.

Minirth, Frank B., and Meier, Paul D. *Happiness Is a Choice: a Manual on the Symptoms, Causes, and Cures of Depression*. Grand Rapids: Baker, 1978.

Nash, Ronald H., ed. *Evangelical Renewal in the Mainline Denominations*. Westchester, IL: Crossway Books, 1987.

Neighbour, Ralph. *The Seven Last Words of the Church*. Nashville: Broadman, 1979.

————— . *This Gift Is Mine*. Nashville: Broadman Films, 1974.

Nouwen, Henri. *Making All Things New: An Invitation to Life in the Spirit*. San Francisco: Harper & Row, 1981.

————— . *The Wounded Healer*. Garden City, NY: Doubleday, 1979.

O'Connor, Elizabeth. *Call to Commitment*. New York: Harper & Row, 1976.

————— . *Journey Inward, Journey Outward*. New York: Harper & Row, 1975.

————— . *The New Community*. New York: Harper & Row, 1976.

Peck, M. Scott. *The Road Less Travelled*. New York: Simon and Schuster, 1980.

Pulkingham, Graham. "A Church Reborn." In *The Spirit and the Church*, pp. 237–244. Compiled by Ralph Martin. New York: Paulist, 1976.

————— . *Gathered For Power*. New York: Morehouse-Barlow, 1972.

————— . *They Left Their Nets*. New York: Morehouse-Barlow, 1973.

Richards, Lawrence O. *Three Churches in Renewal*. Grand Rapids: Zondervan, 1975.

Rood, Wayne. *On Nurturing Christians*. Nashville: Abingdon, 1972.

Schaeffer, Edith. *L'Abri*. Wheaton, IL: Tyndale House, 1972.

————— . *The Tapestry*. Waco: Word, 1985.

Schnackenburg, Rudolf. *The Church in the New Testament*. Translated by W. J. O'Hara. New York: Herder and Herder, 1965.

Smalley, Gary, and Trent, John. *The Blessing*. Nashville: Thomas Nelson, 1986.

Snyder, Howard. "Pietism, Moravianism, and Methodism as Renewal Movements: A Comparative and Thematic Study." Ph.D. dissertation, University of Notre Dame, c. 1979.

————— . *The Problem of Wineskins: Church Renewal in a Technological Age*. Downer's Grove, IL: Inter-Varsity, 1975.

————— . *The Radical Wesley: Pattern for Church Renewal*. Grand Rapids: Zondervan, 1987.

Stevens, R. Paul. *Liberating the Laity*. Downer's Grove, IL: Inter-Varsity, 1985.

Sullivan, Clayton. *Called to Preach, Condemned to Survive: The Education of Clayton Sullivan*. Macon, GA: Mercer, 1985.

Trueblood, D. Elton. *The Company of the Committed.* New York: Harper & Row, 1980.

Verney, Stephen. *Fire in Coventry.* Westwood, NJ: Revell, 1964.

Wagner, C. Peter. *Your Church Can Grow.* Glendale, CA: Regal, 1977.

_____ . *Your Spiritual Gifts Can Help Your Church Grow.* Glendale, CA: Regal, 1979.

Wallis, Jim. *Agenda For Biblical People.* New York: Harper & Row, 1984.

_____ . *Revive Us Again: A Sojourner's Story.* Nashville: Abingdon, 1983.

Webber, Robert. *Evangelicals on the Canterbury Trail.* Waco: Word, 1985.

_____ . *The Majestic Tapestry.* Nashville: Thomas Nelson, 1986.

_____ . *Worship Is a Verb.* Waco: Word, 1985.

_____ . *Worship Old and New.* Grand Rapids: Zondervan, 1982.

Westerhoff, John H. *Will Our Children Have Faith?* New York: Harper & Row, 1983.

Wilke, Richard B. *And Are We Yet Alive? The Future of the United Methodist Church.* Nashville: Abingdon, 1986.

Willimon, William H. "Making Christians in a Secular World." *The Christian Century.* 22 October 1986, pp. 914–917.